I0152842

SOVEREIGN

INSIGHT

"Strength for Your Marriage"

By

Evangelist Naomi Mensah Antwi

Sovereign Insight

Cover by: Entafold Corporation

ISBN: 978-0-692-75305-7
ISBN-10: 0692753052

Email: evangelistnaomi@yahoo.com
Naomi@womenfci.org
Website: www.naomiantwi.com

Give feedback on the book at:
naoantwi@yahoo.com

Printed in U.S.A

I dedicate this book to my darling husband Stephen, my best friend, the love of my life, and my confidant. We both know I could not have done this without you. I'm grateful and I thank you for constantly keeping me sane. ☺
Thank you for supporting me in everything I do and for always standing by me – no matter what Satan throws at us. I am blessed and honored to be your wife.
I thank God for you every day! I love you and May God continues to bless you.
And to our two beautiful, blessed and wonderful children - Princess Aevya and Prince Aeston; I thank God for giving you to us each and every day and I thank you for always putting a smile on my face. You two are awesome blessings to us. And I am grateful to God and proud that even at your young ages, you STILL know how to encourage mommy and daddy on our weakest days. You two are indeed angels sent from God.
May God continue to bless and protect you both now and forever? I love you guys very much.

Thank you God for how far you have brought my Family.

Acknowledgments

I would like to extend my sincere appreciation and gratitude to:

My Heavenly Father – Yahweh – I am a living testimony that NOTHING is too difficult for you. I am truly humbled to be used by you. Thank you for making another book possible.

My husband - Stephen Antwi — the love of my life. Thank you for your continuous support, ideas, encouragement, and prayers. You make me feel like I can do anything. I am blessed to be your wife. I love you.

My Beautiful Children- Princess Aevya & Prince Aeston — I am blessed and honored to be your mother. You are the reason I wake up every morning. I love you very much. May God continue to bless you two.

My Parents — you taught me never to give up. I love you. God bless you.

My Siblings — thank you for helping me realize that I am stronger than I thought. I love you. God bless you all.

My WCI Family – Shay, Gwenn, Gloretta, Vicky, Camille, Star, Cindy - I love you wonderful women of God. I thank God for bringing you ladies into my life. I thank you for your support and prayers. Remember, GOD IS STILL WITH US!

CONTENTS

Please keep in my mind that this book is not intended to be read in a sitting.

Foreword

While running errands, I saw a homeless man in a wheelchair. So I stopped to chat with him. I asked him if he knew God. You know what the man said? This man looked at me and said "**God has been GOOD to me"**.
I couldn't believe it! This man has no home, no job, no money, no food, he is in a **wheelchair** and the only clothes he owns are literally the clothes on his back, he is out on the streets begging strangers for money - yet this homeless man was giving God a heartfelt gratitude!
He was **testifying** to God's greatness! WOW!

This man recognizes the love, mercy and faithfulness of God in his life even though it was obvious that all was not well with him.
I was deeply moved by his words. His words pierced through my heart like a sharp sword. His words made me feel guilty and ashamed because I occasionally find myself complaining about the things I ought to be grateful to God for. His words got me thinking a lot about my own life, everything I have been through and where I am now. And I realized that God has seen me through some pretty tough situations; I have experienced both physical and verbal abuse in relationships.
I remember being in a relationship with a man who made me his daily punching bag; He made sure I got beatings over everything.

If he had a bad day at work, he would take it out on me. If he got angry with someone, I would feel his pain through his punches.
If someone looked at me "the wrong way" he would beat me. I remember how close I came to being homeless myself many times, I can't remember the number of times I have come close to death.
I have experienced more pain to last me a life time and then I thought about how as God has brought me. I thought I had it worse until I met this wonderful - God fearing Homeless man.

I thought a lot about my past and I also thought about stories of friends experiencing the same kind of abuse I suffered, I thought about friends dealing with numerous marital issues and on the verge on divorce. I figured this would be the perfect time for me to help people going through the same struggles and pains I went through.
I made a crucial decision to share some of my painful, hidden and long buried stories with anyone willing to listen. My goal is to use my personal experience to educate anyone who may be going through it right now. If I can help one person out there, if I can save one life, if I can save one marriage, my dream will come true.
For those of us who are always complaining about what we don't have or what we think we need in order to make us whole. For those of us who are never content with our lives, who always wants more, who are always thinking; "if I could just have that new car" or "If I could just have a bigger house, life would be perfect".

This homeless man didn't have even a single room and yet he was testifying God's goodness to me. We seem to have a lot more than this man and yet this man's gratitude to God is greater than ours. The best way we can thank God is to give Him all the glory for everything He has done for us and to help anyone we can help.

Materially speaking, this man has nothing to be proud of, but one thing he definitely has is the **peace of God**. This kind of peace is the **one** thing many of us with all the money in the world don't have and wants badly. The best way to get the peace of God which the bible says "exceeds anything we can understand" and the best way to have God's peace guard our hearts and minds is for us to **live** in Christ Jesus by seeking his will in all we do.

Another One of my favorite Scriptures!
Psalm 86 "A Prayer of King David"

"Bow down Your ear, O LORD, hear me;
For I *am* poor and needy. Preserve my life, for I *am* holy; You are my God; Save Your servant who trusts in You! Be merciful to me, O Lord, For I cry to You all day long. Rejoice the soul of Your servant, For to You, O Lord, I lift up my soul. For You, Lord, *are* good, and ready to forgive, And abundant in mercy to all those who call upon You. Give ear, O LORD, to my prayer; And attend to the voice of my supplications. In the day of my trouble I will call upon You,
For You will answer me. Among the gods *there is* none like You, O Lord; Nor *are there any works* like Your works. All nations whom You have made Shall come and worship before You, O Lord, And shall glorify Your name. For You *are* great, and do wondrous things; You alone *are* God. Teach me Your way, O LORD; I will walk in Your truth;
Unite my heart to fear Your name. I will praise You, O Lord my God, with all my heart,
And I will glorify Your name forevermore. For great *is* Your mercy toward me, And You have delivered my soul from the depths of Sheol.

O God, the proud have risen against me, And a mob of violent *men* have sought my life, And have not set You before them. But You, O Lord, *are* a God full of compassion, and gracious, Longsuffering and abundant in mercy and truth. Oh, turn to me, and have mercy on me! Give Your strength to Your servant, And save the son of Your maidservant. Show me a sign for good, that those who hate me may see *it* and be ashamed, Because You, LORD, have helped me and comforted me". Amen!

Introduction

It takes a split second to make a lifetime decision. It takes a second to decide to steal, murder, fornicate, etc. It takes a second to make a wrong choice. It takes a second to decide to destroy your God-given marriage. It takes a second to get angry and decide to get into a physical fight. It takes a second to dive into any kind of temptation. For some of us, it takes a second for us to be easily influenced by others and to get into some serious troubles.

It takes a second to mess up your entire life. The decisions we make today goes a long way.
But when you think about it, all these "one second" decisions bring about a lifetime of regrets, consequences and punishments.
We must be cautious of the decisions and choices we make today, especially the choices we make within seconds.

They can have deadly consequences. Our decisions shape us. They make or break us. That is why we Christians are blessed to have the **bible**. Our Sovereign **God gives us insight through His word – The bible**. I call that insight "***Sovereign Insight***".

Every Christian must use the bible, as a tool for gaining spiritual wisdom, insight and direction in making life's daily decisions.

We need insight and direction from our Sovereign God in every aspect of our lives. This world has become infested with broken homes caused by divorce. Marriages are rapidly failing and families are falling apart.

I wrote **Sovereign Insight** to encourage marriages, relationships, families, and individuals who are struggling with life's uncertainties, to stay strong and to seek God's direction for their lives.
I have included some of my personal life experiences. Hopefully, you can learn from my mistakes and be motivated by God's presence in those experiences.

Bible says,
"*Today I have given you the choice between life and death, between blessings and curses. Now I call on heaven and earth to witness
the choice you make. Oh, that you would choose life, so that you and your descendants might live! You can make this choice by loving the Lord your God, obeying him, and committing yourself firmly to him. This is the key to your life. And if you love and obey the Lord, you will live long in the land the Lord swore to give your ancestors Abraham, Isaac, and Jacob.*" - Deuteronomy 30:19-20.

Proverbs 3:5-6 tells us to,
"Trust in the LORD with all your heart, do not depend on your own understanding. ***Seek his will in all you do,*** *and he will show you which path to take"*

Before you make any decisions, find out what the word of God says about that particular situation you are experiencing and make sure that your decisions are "in line" with the word of God. Always ask God for spiritual wisdom and insight.

Food for thought:

Our God is a God of RESULTS.

He blows our minds when we least expect it.

He moves ***only*** *when* ***He*** *sees fit - in HIS OWN TIME and ON HIS TERMS.*

Keep in mind that IF God said it, it's FINAL - because His promises are TRUE and His WORD will do just what it is sent out to do...

(Read Psalm 18:30, Isaiah 55:11 and 2 Corinthians 1:20)

PART 1

MARRIAGE

CHAPTER 1

Physical Abuse

Abuse in relationships - whether it's physical abuse or verbal abuse; is a very passionate and sensitive topic for me, because as I have experienced both in my life.

I want to share my personal story with you. This is a story I have buried as part of my past for many years. I feel it's about time I shared it with you – in case you are going through it right now.

Many years ago, I dated an older Ghanaian man. For the purpose of this book, I will refer to him as Jos throughout the story. (Jos is a short version of his real name)

Jos was the kind of man who knew how to put on a great "act" in the presence of other people. Everyone knew him as a "quiet and kind" man. But I knew better. He was charming and sweet in the beginning. Then gradually he became quite jealous and very controlling. At first I thought he was just being protective of me and I found that really sweet and kind of romantic.
To make a long story short, I found myself in a "jobless" situation and I desperately needed a place to stay at the time. Jos suggested that I move into his place until I was able to get back on my feet and though we weren't married, I made the mistake of moving in with him – a decision I regret till this very day.

One day, we had a disagreement and in the middle of our disagreement; he slapped me in the face. I couldn't believe it! I packed up to leave him, but he got on his knees and apologized bitterly. He said it was a mistake, he said he didn't know what came over him; he said he didn't mean to hit me and promised never to hit me again.
Silly me; I believed him. So I stayed.

But the beatings didn't stop there. It continued and got worse every time.
I got beatings over every little thing.

If he had a bad day at work, he would take it out on me when he got home. If he got angry with someone outside, I would feel his pain through his punches the minute he got home.
The beatings escalated rather rapidly and only got worse. I was always hiding bruises at school and among friends.
Of course he would apologize every time and do something "nice" for me afterwards.
And then he would promise never to do it again. The promise was good until he gets upset again over **something – anything.**
He would beat me for every little thing – using his hands or using whatever he could lay his hands on. I once confided in a female friend I had met in school and told her everything about my abusive relationship. She advised me to leave Jos at once. But that night when I went home, Jos was so nice and sweet; he even apologized to me and promised to never hit me again. He even told me how much he loved me and as young and naive as I was, I believed him.

The funny thing was that, somehow, I always made excuses for him. I made myself responsible for his actions. Can you believe that?
I always thought maybe if I changed certain things about myself, he would quit beating me.
I always thought I made him do it, because his apologies always began with "I am sorry but..."
Two days later, he started hitting me again.
I wasn't allowed to even greet any man who wasn't a "known" relative.

If he caught a man glancing in my direction, I would get punished for that at home.
We were once invited to an "all-black" party. When we got there, a male childhood friend I hadn't seen in years greeted me with a huge hug. Jos got furious, dragged me out of the party and threw me into his car and drove off.
He threw insults at me the whole drive home. When we got home, he dragged me upstairs to his apartment on the third floor, opened the door and threw me onto the floor inside the apartment. Of course, the whole time showering more insults on me. The beatings started.
He was so angry that he picked up a dining room chair and threw it at me. In my attempt to prevent the chair from hitting my face, I tried to block the chair using my left palm.

A huge piece of wood from the chair went straight through the inside of my left palm and blood started gushing out. Low and behold the neighbors had called the police.
When the police knocked on the door, he started begging me to change the story and when I said no, he got on his knees and swore never to hit me again – with tears streaming down his cheeks.

I felt sorry for him and guilty at the same time for **making** him angry. Can you imagine that?
Like I said, I was naïve, young and stupid.
Meanwhile, my hand was still gushing out blood, my dress was drenched with my blood,

I was in serious pain and the police didn't give up - they kept knocking on the door even louder and shouting "police - open the door".
So when I finally opened the door, there were two cops at the door. When the police asked me if everything was okay, I lied and answered yes.
I had held my left hand behind my back and the carpet was soaking wet with blood. I kept trying to force a smile and said everything was fine.

They asked what was going on and asked to see my hand (because they could see the blood dripping on the carpet as I held my hand behind me).
I showed them my hand and told them I had accidentally cut myself while cooking.
They looked at Jos and back at me (twice) and asked if I was sure that was what happened and I lied again and said yes.
They asked whether I needed paramedics and I said I was on my way to the emergency room.
They asked whether Jos had touched me, one of the cops assured me that I could tell them the truth.
But again, I lied and said he didn't touch me.
So the cops finally left.

Jos took me to the emergency room, where I gave the same story to the medical personnel.
I got stitches that night and they also placed a cast on my hand along with a sling over my neck to hold my hand in place. I still have the scar inside my left palm to show for it.

After I got out of the hospital, I had nowhere to go, so when he showed up at the hospital to take me home and begged me again, I went home with him.
For the first time in my life, I started thinking and thinking hard about everything I was going through.
My ordeal reminded me of my auntie back home from my mother's side of the family, who had been blind for as long as I could remember.

I remembered asking my mum one day, about how my auntie got blind and I remembered my mum telling me that my aunt had suffered a lot of beatings from an abusive boyfriend and one of those beatings had rendered her blind forever while the abusive boyfriend moved on to marry another woman.
I realized right there and then that I **had** to get out of that relationship or I would one day end up inside a casket, deformed or disable.

Although I didn't have a place to go and I didn't really know how I was going to make it without him, I managed to leave him.
I was not prayerful at the time so prayer was the last thing on my mind.
I waited for Jos to leave for work and I gathered the courage and strength and I packed up my stuff and left him. He chased me everywhere, begging and promising to change.
But this time, my mind was made up. This time I had made a firm decision to love "ME" more.

This time, I refused to feel responsible for his actions. I stayed away from him.
My friend, abuse comes in various forms, shapes and sizes. There's physical abuse, verbal, emotional, psychological, sexual, etc.
I have experienced both physical and verbal abuse and I can tell you from my experience personal that an abusive person never changes.

An abusive partner or spouse might apologize and may even show remorse, but trust me when I tell you that, that first or second hit will only increase to third, fourth, fifth hit and many more hits. They will end up physically deforming you or rendering you permanently disabled - if you don't leave them. Eventually, the hits will graduate to murder. An abusive partner will never change because they don't know love and they don't know God.

They are full of themselves and some of them are mentally deranged and need serious help.
But since you are not a clinical psychologist, a psychiatrist or a psychotherapist, it is not your job to help them.
The fact is that you are their punching bag and you must save yourself and pray for them. If you are not careful, you will lose your life in the process of "helping them".
Because they don't know how to love themselves, they can't possibly love anyone. And you are not the right person to teach them what they don't know.

It is said that "you cannot tame a grown dog" Consider the fact that, even though you **think** you are in love with them, you MUST be more **in love with YOU** and leave at once! Leave before it's too late. A person who truly loves you can't bear to see you in pain. They claim to love you and yet they take pleasure in hurting you physically and/or emotionally. **That** is **not** "love" my dear friend.

Bible says in 1 John 4:8 that,
"He who does not love does not know God, for God is love"
Many people wonder and I know you are wondering too;
Why do women stay in abusive relationships?
Why don't they just leave?
Well for me, I stayed because at first, I thought he loved me and I kept on believing he'll change.
I also felt sorry for him for some reason.
And then, after a while I started feeling like I wouldn't make it without him. I also began feeling responsible **for what he was doing to me**.

I know it sounds crazy, but I thought somehow it was my fault. I remember reporting him to his mum one time, but she saw her son's abuse as "normal" because most African mothers from the old generation were "okay" with men abusing women. I was told back in the day, physical abuse was the norm for most of our mothers and grandmothers. I tried calling the police a few times too, but he told me that if the police showed up, they would have taken me away because I was living in his apartment.

Yeah. I know. I believed him.
Did I mention I was young, naïve and stupid at the time? ☺
I have been through a lot in my life time and I will cover some of those experiences in my future books. But I can confidently tell you that, everything I have been through has made me stronger, wiser and smarter.
My life experiences have actually made me appreciate God and his many blessings in my life even more. I feel like I can now handle just about anything and now with God as my solid rock, there's just no challenger!
Other women may have different reasons why they stayed in abusive relationships.
But if you are reading this book, and you happen to be in an abusive relationship, I pray that God will grant you the courage and grace to get out of it. Please get out before it's too late.
There's no reason under the sun to justify you staying with such a person.

Trust me, it's not love and it's not worth it.
If you don't leave, soon or later, one of you will die and **he** will not be the one dying.
My friend, get out now!
Don't allow that person to abuse you any longer.
Bible says;
"Don't you realize that your body is the temple of the Holy Spirit, who lives in you and was given to you by God? You do not belong to yourself, for God bought you with a high price. So you must honor God with your body" - 1 Corinthians 6:19-2.

You were made in the image of God.
You are precious and the apple of God's eyes.
So don't allow anyone to abuse you.

1 Peter 2:9 says;
"But you are a chosen generation, a royal priesthood, a holy nation, and His own special people, that you may proclaim the praises of Him who called you out of darkness into His marvelous light"

Your heavenly father holds you in a very high esteem. It's about time you start seeing yourself as valuable as God sees you.

Ask God for the courage, grace and strength to walk out of that relationship before it's too late.

At the end of the day, YOU MATTER. Make your life count. You deserve to be treated like beautiful the queen that you are. Refuse to accept anything less!
If I had stayed in the relationship with Jos, I don't think we will be having this conversation right now.
If I had stayed with him, I wouldn't have been able to meet my very wonderful husband.

Before you cry "Abuse"...

If you are a man; what you are about to read is not an excuse for you to abuse your woman in any way. So don't get your hopes up.
That being said, I know there are some very physically abusive men out there and unfortunately, some of us have either dated one, married to one or are currently dealing with one as I speak. Some of us are even making excuses for their actions. But not all men are physically or even verbally abusive. There are actually some really good men out there!

There are true gentlemen out there too, and they are very respectful of women, very gentle, caring, loving and **manly** at the same time.
I would know – I have experienced both side of the fence. I have dated a physically abusive kind, I have also dated the verbally abusive kind and by God's grace, I am now married to one of the **really great ones**! So, Trust me, I know.

I also know there are many verbally abusive **women** out there, and believe it or not, some of these women can get physically abusive with their men too. I have witnessed a few.

The thing is; many times, the good men end up with the bad women and vice-versa. Unfortunately, a physically abusive woman will end up with a great guy who would rather walk away than hit a woman - no matter what she does to him.

I have seen a few women trying to turn their men into abusive men by being physically abusive themselves. What do I mean by that?
Great question.
Well, let me give you an example of what I am talking about; I met a couple who fought a lot. And every time they had an argument, the lady would literally get all up in her husband's face. She would push the guy, scratch his face, tear his shirt, and ask him to beat her. She would say to him "beat me, beat me, aren't you a man?'...
And if her husband tried to walk away, she would grab him, scratch his back, hit him and start breaking everything she could get her hands on – including furniture. She would throw things at him.

I know you are probably imagining the lady being "bigger and taller" than the man. Nope.
She was a beautiful small and petite woman and he was a "big and tall" man.
If this man wasn't a patient person, what do you suppose would have happened?

You guessed right. He would probably have hit her eventually and he would have regretted it later, because he wasn't the abusive kind. But this man exercised great patience and never once touched his wife. He always found a way to walk away from her.

The abuse finally trumped their love for each other and they ended up getting a divorce. Luckily, they had no children.

Can you imagine the psychological and emotional effect it would have had on their children?
What I am describing doesn't only happen in romantic relationships.

It happens in many relationships like friendships and acquaintances between a man and a woman.
I watched a story in the news a few months ago and the story was about a female who grabbed a man in the arm forcibly. But when the man also grabbed her forcibly, she began accusing him of physical abuse. Yes, a man shouldn't hit a woman under any circumstance. But if you hit your fellow woman, how many women would not retaliate?

Some women have the tendency of intentionally **provoking, pushing and tempting** a man to hit them. When they finally succeed in getting beat up by that man, they begin to cry "abuse".
Before you cry abuse, ask yourself a few questions; did you hit him first? Who started the physical abuse?
I have **seen** some women who were so quick to slap their men over a little argument. Yes, some men exercise control and refuse retaliate.
But what if the man you slapped decides to slap you back?
I bet you would start crying "abuse".
Again, my question is who started the abuse?

By now, you are probably thinking "Evangelist Naomi is condoning and encouraging physical abuse".
That is not what I am doing.

I want every woman to understand that being a woman entails way more than "playing the woman card" when it conveniences us.

You have to understand that whether you have children or not, whether you are an older woman or a younger woman - some younger person other than yourself is always watching your actions. Whether you like it or not, someone out there has made you their role model. Whether you know it or not, someone looks up to you in the most remarkable way.
You must let them see what "being a true strong woman" is about.

Think about it, we now live in the 21st century, and in this century women **can and are** allowed to do whatever men can do.
In this century, women have not been restricted to being just; "House wives, cooks, cleaners and mothers" - like the generations of women before us. On the contrary, we have been empowered to "do it all" and **still** be very successful in life.

We are called to be submissive to our husbands – yes – but we have also been called for greater purpose, which is to **partner** with our husbands.

Proverbs 31 refers to a good wife as "*A Wife of Noble Character". Bible calls a good wife "strong and energetic, a hard worker". It describes her further, it says; "Her husband can trust her, and she will greatly enrich his life.*

Proverbs 31 continues to say "She brings him good, not harm, all the days of her life" and here's one of my favorites; "There are many virtuous and capable women in the world, ***but you surpass them all!"***

A proverbs 31 woman is bold, calm, and submissive and **partners** with her husband through prayers and in everything.
Women are holding high, powerful and important office across the globe. Women are equally very strong in this century.
But when a woman goes out of her way to hit and physically abuse a man, it is automatically allowed by society and everyone expects the man to endure it. And when a man is forced to defend himself from a woman's abuse, suddenly, she cries "abuse" and everyone throws a fit. So the man gets into trouble. I think we all agree that physical abuse along with any other form of abuse must stop now! Physical abuse should never be tolerated from both men and women.
An abusive woman must change her ways.
Don't hit with the intension to blame the man for your actions.

We (women) are always demanding "gender equality", we want to receive equal treatment just like the men, we do not want to be discriminated against based on our gender, and yet we hold the men to a double-standard.
No one should be subjected to an abuse of any kind; especially physical abuse - it is not good for anyone – man or woman. It is unacceptable.

When it comes to physical or verbal abuse, you must abide by two rules; do not hit and do not do name-calling. If you are blessed enough to find a good man, please hold onto him and don't forcibly turn him into an abusive man.
Don't forget "the golden rule", Bible strongly advises us in Luke 6:31 to "***do to others as you would like them to do to you***".

It's really very simple; do not hit your man and if he is a true gentleman, he will treat you like the queen you are. As I stated earlier, I have experienced both sides of the fence. And I can tell you that – "good men" and true "gentle men" are very hard find and very rare. If God chooses to bring you a good man, please don't push him away, don't mistaken his patience and love for weakness.

I know some women don't mean to be physically abusive. They feel the need to push their man into treating them badly because of what they may have been through with another man prior to getting into their current relationship - they themselves are coming from another relationship where their previous man physically abused them, therefore they are not used to being treated with love and respect. They are used to being abused.

They now see being "kicked around" and being insulted as "love".
So they become the "abuser" in the new relationship.

If you are going through what I just described, I strongly suggest you get in the habit of being prayerful and please get some help by seeing a clinical psychiatrist. You need help and that man can't help you. You will only end up destroying your marriage if you don't get some help.

Keep in mind that some men are not abusive, but they **will not** tolerate an abuse from their woman either. They **will** either retaliate or leave you one day.

Although Bible tells us to turn the other cheek when we are slapped, even most women do not oblige to that advice– most women will hit you back. In the same way, some good men might hit you back - eventually.

If you have the habit of hitting the men you date or your husband, I will advise you to change now, because if you don't quit, don't cry "abuse" when your man defends himself one day with retaliation.

A woman wants to be loved and respected, not only as a woman - but as a person.
A true woman does not want to be dealt with based on "gender" but rather based on who they are as a person.

In the same way, we must remember that respect must be earned and not demanded. If you respect yourself and you respect others, chances are most people you interact with, will have no choice **but** to respect you too.

Bible tells husbands to,
"*Give honor to their wives*" - 1 Peter 3:7.

In the same Bible tells us - women in 1 Peter 3:1-6,
"*In the same way, you wives must accept the authority of your husbands. Then, even if some refuse to obey the Good News, your godly lives will speak to them without any words. They will be won over by observing your pure and reverent lives. Don't be concerned about the outward beauty of fancy hairstyles, expensive jewelry, or beautiful clothes. You should clothe yourselves instead with the beauty that comes from within, the unfading beauty of a gentle and quiet spirit, which is so precious to God. This is how the holy women of old made themselves beautiful. They put their trust in God and accepted the authority of their husbands. For instance, Sarah obeyed her husband, Abraham, and called him her master. You are her daughters when you do what is right without fear of what your husbands might do*"

As I always say, you must give respect in order to be respected. Respect your man and if he is one of the good men out there, you will experience a beautiful marriage filled with love and happiness. I wish you a happy marriage filled with grace, love and respect.

Verbal Abuse

Most couples fight a lot. But when the fight turns into various name-callings, when you begin calling each other every bad name one can think of - ignoring the fact that you are doing so in public, with friends, family or strangers as witnesses, something's got to give.
When a man can easily hurl very embarrassing insults at his wife and the woman can easily do the same, something is dangerously amiss in that marriage.
Married couples fight and curse at each other right in front of their children too.
I can't understand **how** a person can call his or her spouse – **whom they claim to love** - all kinds of terrible names, and then **claim** that person as "**my** wife" or "**my** husband"!
How can a married couple so blatantly **disrespect** each other so much **and** in **public**?
How can you not have any respect for the man or woman you claim to **love**?
It makes absolutely no sense!

A strong and happy marriage **requires respect** from **both** parties. Respect is essential in every marriage, especially if you have children.

Your children are LEARNING from mom and dad! By fighting and cursing at each other in front of your children, you are teaching them that marriage is supposed to be just like that.
The husband is teaching the son that a woman is to be treated just like that – with total disrespect and abuse.

The wife is teaching the daughter that a woman is to be treated like trash and that a woman is supposed to ACT like trash.
You are both setting your children up to FAIL.
Because of you, they will never experience the joy of marriage even if they meet a good partner.

By God's grace, my husband and I have been married for over eleven years.
Do we have a perfect marriage? No.
Do we fight? Absolutely
But he does not beat me, I don't beat him and we don't call each other names - no matter how angry we make each other. We always manage to get our points across without insulting each other.

And with God's help, you can also get your point across without the name-calling.
A good, happy and successful marriage requires the word of God in order to function properly.
You can start by **praying for spiritual maturity** and grace for both of you.

You must **ask** God to step into your marriage and take total control of your marriage and family.
Ask God for patience.

The devil can never destroy a **praying couple and a praying family**.

So be prayerful always.

James 4:2 says,
'*You don't have what you want because you don't ask God for it"*

Bible commands husbands to RESPECT their wives in Colossians 3:19,
"Husbands, love your wives and never treat them harshly"

1 Peter 3:7 also states;
"*You husbands must give honor to your wives. Treat your wife with understanding as you live together. She may be weaker than you are, but she is your equal partner in God's gift of new life. Treat her as you should so your prayers will not be hindered*'

The same Bible also says,
"*Each man must love his wife as he loves himself, and the wife must respect her husband.*"
- Ephesians 5:33.

1 Corinthians 11:11 clearly states that,
"*Women are not independent of men, and men are not independent of women.*"

It will take both husband and wife to make the relationship work. **A happy home will require the word of God, respect and efforts from both of you**.

RESPECT is essential for a healthy and happy marriage. It doesn't matter how angry you get, please control your tongue!
Never insult your partner.
They are your soul mates.

You two became ONE the minute you said "I do". So if you insult him or her, you are really insulting yourself. And you are insulting the God who put you together.

Respecting Yourself

I want to elaborate on how we "treat each other" as people. I don't understand a few things in this generation.
For example: A woman constantly refers to herself as a "bitch" either in anger or in a friendly chat with her friends. Yet she gets angry and offended when someone else refers to her as such.
A black person (man/woman) has no problem referring to themselves as a "nigger". Yet they get offended and upset when someone else calls them by that VERY NAME they "gave" to themselves.
A person (man/woman) sleeps around – literally with anyone willing to sleep with them, yet they are shocked when someone refers to them as "prostitute or a whore" (and yes, that name applies to men too).

And then we have others who are always so quick to use cursing words like the "F" and "B" words and so on. But they don't understand that, by using those very words, they are also opening the door and inviting others to equally disrespect them. Keep in mind that RESPECT is EARNED. You can't give "disrespect" and expect "respect" in return. You can't rate yourself an "F" and expect others to rate you an "A". You can't place yourself in the cutter and expect people to place you inside a palace. Unfortunately, life does not work like that.
People will treat you exactly how YOU treat yourself and how you treat them.

People will treat you how you allow them to treat you. People will treat you according to how you carry yourself.
Some of us have such low self-esteem that we don't think **much** of ourselves. Yet we expect others to think **much** of us.
How can you not think much of yourself?
How can you so easily disrespect yourself?
How can you hold yourself in such low-esteem?
How can you set low expectations for yourself?
How can you misuse your body in any way?
How can you call yourself a "bitch"? Really?!

YOU have been SO FEARFULLY AND WONDERFULLY MADE by YAHWEH HIMSELF?
Do you not know that God MADE YOU in His OWN IMAGE?
Oh, my dear friends, don't you know how PRECIOUS YOU ARE to God??...
Bible says, God carefully made all the delicate, inner parts of YOUR BODY and knit YOU together in your mother's womb.
YES, He made YOU SO WONDERFULLY complex! You are far more precious than rubies. Treat yourself as such.

God's WORKMANSHIP IS MARVELOUS, you should know this, because YOU ARE HIS WORKMANSHIP!!...
If you don't believe me, read Psalm 139.
Behave like the Prince and Princesses that you are - for OUR Father is THE King of ALL Kings, who made YOU in His own image.

Don't forget that, People will treat you according to the way you carry yourself. Your spouse will respect you if you respect yourself enough to respect him.

"Long after Abraham, Isaac, and Jacob had died, God said to Moses, 'I am the God of Abraham, the God of Isaac, and the God of Jacob. So he is the God of the living, not the dead. You have made a serious error."

- Mark 12:26-27 -

Your words

There are times when we get upset with our loved ones. During those times, most of us say a lot of negative things and unleash insults on them. Some of us say many things "out of anger" - things we should never say to our spouses, children, partners, siblings, friends or even enemies. Remember: **Though the tongue is a tiny part of the body, it's also the most powerful tool in the body**. Bible states that,
"*The tongue is a small thing that makes grand speeches. But a tiny spark can set a great forest on fire*"...James 3:5.

Our own tongues can either bless or curse us by the things we spill out of our mouths.
We are all guilty of saying things out of anger. But I want to focus on those of us who are MARRIED. Satan hates marriage, so be rest assured that he WILL catch and HOLD onto every negative word that you say to your spouse about your marriage.

You must begin CONTROLLING your tongue - especially with regards to your marriage.
You must NOT **enable**, encourage or assist the devil in sabotaging your marriage.
Don't make Satan's work easy at all.

You MUST ALWAYS PRAY for God's forgiveness, grace, direction and protection on your marriage and family.

Pray with Me,

King of Glory I thank you for your mercies that are new every morning for me and my family.
Thank you for blessing me with family.
Thank you for my marriage.
Most High God, please forgive me for all my sins.
Daddy, please **cancel every negative** word I have uttered against my spouse and against my marriage. Please FIX whatever may be broken in my marriage.
I use the Powerful BLOOD of Jesus Christ to CANCEL every negative thing I have said about my marriage.
God, please help me to CONTROL my tongue moving forward.
Lord, please BLESS my marriage, BLESS me, BLESS my spouse and BLESS my family!
In the mighty name of Jesus I pray!
AMEN!!

When you get too angry to talk, ask God for the grace and patience to remain SILENT.

My mum used to tell me, "Naomi, when you get too angry and you don't have anything good to say, walk away from the situation or put water in your mouth and hold it in like a bubble until you calm down before spitting it out or swallowing it".

That was a great advice. Try it some time.
It actually works!

CHAPTER 2

Commitment

Marriage begins with a decision to love, respect, and commit to the other person. Marriage is when two people with different backgrounds and sometimes from different cultures, falls in love with each other and make a **decision** to be joined together as **one**.

When God created marriage, He intended for marriage to be a lifetime commitment between a man and a woman.

So when these two people tie the knot by saying "I do", they are really making a solid and holy commitment to God and to each other.
That means you only have eyes for your spouse and no one else. That means you do not pack your bags every time there's a misunderstanding or disagreement. That means you keep other people out of your marital affairs. That means your siblings, parents and friends do not get to dictate nor decide what transpires in your marriage.

When Stephen and I first got married, I didn't really understand the true meaning of the word "marriage". I would pack my bags and threaten to leave every time we had a little misunderstanding. I did that in the early stages of our marriage. Until I realized that if I keep threatening to leave, my husband might just oblige one day. ☺
I also realized that I was inviting Satan into my marriage every time I threatened my marriage.

Genesis 2:18 says,
"Then the Lord God said, "It is not good for the man to be alone. I will make a helper who is just right for him."

Marriage should never be entered lightly or for the wrong reason. As I always say, marriage is hard enough with a spouse you love.
Marrying for any other reason other than love, can only result in a dangerous disaster for both parties involved.

Marriage is not an item you can easily return to the store for "exchange or return" purposes after purchase and should never be treated as such.
A committed marriage should make prayer a number priority.
You must have God at the beginning of the marriage, in the middle of the marriage, at the root of the marriage and behind the marriage.
If you keep God out of your marriage, divorce will happen - fail sooner or later. If your spouse is not a Christian, your goal should be to win his or her soul through prayer and the word.

Apostle Paul stated in 1 Corinthians 7:12:14,

"If a fellow believer has a wife who is not a believer and she is willing to continue living with him, he must not leave her. And if a believing woman has a husband who is not a believer and he is willing to continue living with her, she must not leave him. For the believing wife brings holiness to her marriage, and the believing husband brings holiness to his marriage".

Another key tool to staying committed in your marriage is choosing to love your spouse - **unconditionally**. Make a decision to accept him or her for "who they are". Do not try to change them. There is a saying that "you can't tame a grown dog".
Before you even consider marrying that person, you should already **know** that person inside and out.

I know you can't really know a person 100%, but you should know enough about them before you "tie the knot". There is no reason for you to try to change them after you get married. Never marry someone with the intention to "change" them.

Problems arise in many marriages when a spouse tries desperately to change his/her partner into being someone else.
For example; prior to getting married, a lady knew very well that her fiancé was lazy. She knew her man would rather not work - not because he couldn't find a job, he just refuses to work.
She knew this the entire dating period, because he never pretended to be anything different.

Another lady knew that her boyfriend wasn't the romantic type; she knew her man doesn't "open doors", "buy roses", she knew her man will never send her a text in the middle of the day just to say "I love you", she knew him well, and although she prefers the romantic type for a husband, she settles for him by saying yes to his marriage proposal – with the intention to "change" him one day.

These two ladies **knew** their men very well before they said "I do", but after getting married, they suddenly want to change them.
The men refuse to change based on a very legitimate fact; ***their women knew and accepted them before the marriage.***

So that raises the million-dollar question;
Why are they now complaining and fighting with their husbands over the same red flags they wholeheartedly accepted **before** they got married. The reason is that, most people get married with the intention to change their partners.
But changing someone you love, into someone else is simply impossible and definitely not worth it. Accept them for who they are and love them anyway or don't marry them at all.

Commitment means you **stay** in the marriage through thick and thin. You stay whether fiancés are good or bad. You stay whether your spouse is sick or not. Commitment means you do not allow others to mingle in your marital affairs.
That means you do not bad-mouth your spouse to third-parties.
You cannot have a happy marriage without love.
As I said earlier, marriage in itself is very hard.
That is why it requires true love, selflessness, patience, endurance, forgiveness, tolerance and commitment.

The word of God clearly indicates that love is from God.
1 John 4:8 says,

"*But anyone who does not love does not know God, for God is love.*"

Loving your spouse means being there when he or she needs you, it means supporting and standing by your spouse under any circumstance, it means making your spouse your number one priority and being loyal to them.

For example; if your spouse had both legs when you first got married and years later he gets into an accident and loses one leg, you don't pack up and leave the marriage. And you do not stay in the marriage only to maltreat him/her.
You remain in the marriage and show your spouse more love, by taking good care of him/her.
Real love is through "**thick and thin**",
"In happiness and in sadness" "In good health and in bad health" "Whether rich or poor."
Love is when you **stay no matter what** - not as an obligation, but because of the love you have for your spouse.

Loving your spouse means staying faithful to God and your spouse. Loving your spouse means praying constantly **for** your spouse and praying **with** your spouse.

Psalm 127:1 states;
"Unless the LORD builds a house, the work of the builders is wasted. Unless the LORD protects a city, guarding it with sentries will do no good."

Please understand that you and your spouse are two sinners who have been brought together by God Almighty **as one**.
Bible says "For ALL have sinned and fallen short of the glory of God".
You and your spouse are both **imperfect.** So don't expect perfection from your spouse, because there is no way you can give perfection.
Don't hold him or her to higher standards than you hold yourself. Be prayerful, patient, humble and ready to forgive.

Bible says in Ephesians 4:2-3,
"Always be humble and gentle. Be patient with each other, making allowance for each other's faults because of your love. Make every effort to keep yourselves united in the Spirit, binding yourselves together with peace."

If your love is genuine and solid for each other, no one can come between the two of you.
And **together**, you can be stronger in the Lord.

Bible says in Ecclesiastes 4:12;
"A person standing alone can be attacked and defeated, but two can stand back-to-back and conquer"
1 Peter 4:8 also states,
"Most important of all, continue to show deep love for each other, for love covers a multitude of sins."

When you are **in love** with your spouse, you can't stay away from him or her too long and you can't stand to see them in pain or unhappy.

The most beautiful marriage is a couple who have been married for ages and yet their love for each other remains stronger and deeper than ever before. True love equals happy marriage, happy home and happy family. True love conquers ALL. Make a firm commitment today. Make a commitment to love your spouse and to be happy in your marriage no matter what. Commit to success in all you do. **Commit to trust God fully and together** - no matter what.

Never allow fear of failure, discouragement, anything or **anyone** to cloud your view of the future God has planned for you and your family. Commit to move ahead no matter what and despite the odds. Trust God for the impossible. And whatever you do, please don't forget that the **key** to your spiritual and physical success is **prayer**. The key to uproot the spirit of divorce, separation, confusion, fights and unnecessary heartache is **prayer.**
PRAY about everything and pray TOGETHER. That way, you can continue to have the favor of God in your marriage and family.
Do not worry about **anyone or anything**. Keep your eyes on God alone. Keep moving TOGETHER.
Once you get married, "I" become "us".

Nehemiah 6:16 says;
"*When our enemies and the surrounding nations heard about it, they were frightened and humiliated. They realized this work had been done with the help of our God*".

Division in the Family

You must understand that not everyone has your best interest at heart and not everyone wants to see you happy. Your friend's marriage may seem beautiful and "happy" from the outside, but in reality her marriage might be more rocky and a very unhappy one - than yours. She may be pretending to have a happy and wonderful marriage than she truly does.

When such a friend gets closer to your family and sees that you and your spouse are truly happy, when they see the kind of relationship you have with your spouse, when they see the genuine love and affection you two share, when they see how "natural" things *flows* between you and your spouse, they get **jealous**. When they see the beautiful relationship your spouse has with your children, they get even more jealous, because their spouse never hangs out with their children.

Instead of being happy for you, they begin planning, strategizing, and plotting to destroy your family. They start by creating and causing confusion between you and your spouse. They will even involve anyone who is willing to listen. They will form a team of members to rally against you. You'd be surprised to know how many years of planning some of these self-appointed "enemies of your marriage" have been operating in the shadows - all the while pretending to love you. If you are not careful, they will cause a great division in your family.

People like that can even turn your own children against you. If you are not a true Christian, if your love and trust for each other is not strong enough, if you don't have a good communication relationship within your family - they will succeed in breaking your family up.

After one of my fasting and prayers, I remember how amazingly God exposed a couple of people who had been working vigorously in the shadows against my marriage for twelve years!
Honestly, I can't say I was shocked, because God had been showing me a lot of different red flags over the years, but I had convinced myself that one of them cared about me.
By giving them the benefits of doubt, I lost guard and allowed one of them into my comfort zone. But God was watching them the entire time and protecting my family from their evil plans.

As I was saying, not everyone has your best interest at heart and not everyone wants to see you happy.
You must be mindful of the people you open up to.
Be mindful of who you bring into your home.
Be careful of the kind of people you seek advice from and be very careful of the kind of advice you are taking when it comes to your marriage and family.

Bible says, "The human heart is the most deceitful of all things, and desperately wicked.
Who really knows how bad it is?" Jeremiah 17:9

Only God knows what's inside the human heart. Love everyone around you, but don't be too trusting of people.
Remember what Samuel said; "He said God doesn't look at things like humans do. Humans see only what is visible to the eyes, but the Lord sees into the heart."

For this reason, you must never stop praying for your family. The more you pray for your spouse and kids, the farther your true enemies of progress will be drifted away from your family. When you serve God diligently, He protects you and your family from the wicked and unseen plans of your enemies. He protects you especially from theses enemies moonlighting as your friends.

Don't allow anyone to influence you negatively against your spouse or against your children. If anything, **you** must influence them positively.

No one can divide your family unless you let them.

One of my favorite Scriptures!

"O Sovereign LORD, you have only begun to show your greatness and the strength of your hand to me, your servant. Is there any god in heaven or on earth who can perform such great and mighty deeds as you do?"

***** Deuteronomy 3:24 *****

Power of Transparency

Transparency is a MUST in a marriage in order for the marriage is to survive. Transparency is defined in the Webster dictionary as "honest and open: not secretive".
"Transparency and honesty" means; being "open" with your spouse about **everything**.
It means no keeping secrets, no manipulations, no hiding of anything from your spouse. If you feel the need to hide something, you probably shouldn't do that thing to begin with.
It means talking more with your spouse than to a third-party.

There's just no way of building a true and meaningful bond with your spouse without being transparent with each other.
Keeping secrets, telling lies, hiding crucial and relevant information from your spouse can be costly and deadly in a relationship. Transparency is a huge cause of broken relationships. Keeping secrets from each other opens the door of your marriage to your enemies.
Stephen and I decided in the early stages of our relationship to be transparent to each other.
We made transparency an integral part of our relationship. Till this day, we tell each other EVERYTHING. There have been times in the past when we "occasionally" made the mistake of withholding information from each other, but we quickly rectified that mistake by being forthcoming.

I never do anything without informing Stephen and He never does anything without informing me either. Transparency has made our marriage stronger.

For example; there was a time when someone decided to "light a fire" into our marriage in hopes of breaking us up. Her first step was to attack me with false accusations, accompanied by insults and when that didn't work, she went to my husband and loaded him with many lies about me. This woman made up a bunch of stuff - you wouldn't believe the stuff she **claimed** I did and said. Some of her made-up stories were extremely sensitive things that could've easily broken most marriages.
But what she didn't know was that my husband and I share everything and our marriage was arranged by God Himself. She wasn't aware of the fact that my husband and I don't keep secrets from each other. Because my husband **knows** me well, Stephen automatically **knew** her claims were all lies. I **didn't need** to explain myself any further. Do you see my point?

By God's grace, she failed miserably in her quest to destroy my marriage.

I can confidently tell you that God, in his own grace, saved my marriage through "transparency", from whatever was "cooked up" against me.

Transparency is not always convenient and it is certainly not easy, but it is **vital** in every marriage and in every relationship. Besides, if your life is an open-book, you should have nothing to worry about.

As long as you practice transparency in your marriage, no one can shoot "lies or sound-bites" into your spouse's heart - against you. No one can plant evil seeds in your marriage, and no one can come between you and your spouse.

Honesty and transparency are very important in every marriage. A transparent marriage is greater and stronger than anything you can ever imagine. Give your spouse the privilege of knowing "ALL" of you.

Allow him or her to KNOW YOU well.
Be transparent and honest.
Commit to transparency and honesty in your relationship.

A word of advice on "being transparent"
This practice has worked for me;

Give your spouse the "benefit of doubt" - no matter how tough and horrible the truth may sound.
Tell yourself that "this is hard to deal with, but this person is **still being forthcoming** about it with me".
They are being "open" with you - **let it count.**
Do not crucify them for it.
Do not make them regret it.
If the truth is too difficult for you to handle, ask God to step in and give you the grace and wisdom you need for both of you to pull through – **together**.

It is true that the truth sometimes hurt, but in my experience, knowing the hurtful truth – upfront - is far better than being told a beautiful lie and then discovering the truth later.
When a lie comes before the truth, it breaks **trust** and creates an irreparable damage to the marriage.
But even if the truth is hard to take in, chances are, you two might pull through just fine.
And after the storm of pain comes a love stronger than steel and an unbreakable happy marriage.

Transparency bring Trials

Transparency sometimes brings trials into the marriage. But you must stay strong, relentless and committed to your marriage. You must trust and hold onto God's power. When God asked Abraham to sacrifice his only son, whom he loves dearly — a son he had to wait forever to get from the same God, Abraham didn't hesitate.
In fact, Abraham prepared his son for the sacrifice the next day.

Genesis 22:6-8 says;
"*So Abraham placed the wood for the burnt offering on Isaac's shoulders, while he himself carried the fire and the knife. As the two of them walked on together, Isaac turned to Abraham and said, "Father?" "Yes, my son?" Abraham replied. "We have the fire and the wood," the boy said, "but where is the sheep for the burnt offering?" "God will provide a sheep for the burnt offering, my son," Abraham answered. And they both walked on together*"

Abraham was actually going to kill his son just because God said so!
But here's what I love about the story;
verse 11 says, at that moment the angel of the Lord called to Abraham from heaven and told him not to lay a hand on the boy.

And God PROVIDED a ram for the sacrifice - just as Abraham trusted Him to do.

God didn't want the boy killed; God was only testing Abraham's faith in Him.
As you know, Abraham passed the test with flying colors. What's the connection? **Trust in God**.
God brought you and your spouse together as one; don't be afraid to be transparent and honest with your spouse. Trust that when trials and problems arise, that same God will see you through.
You only need to hang on long enough to pass the faith test.

I don't know what problem you are facing in your marriage, but perhaps God is testing how committed you are to Him, your spouse and your faith in Him. Hold on in faith long enough to pass the test.
For after passing the test, come unimaginable miracles in your family.

CHAPTER 3

Finances

I decided to do a little survey about finances in marriage. So I spoke with a few women. One woman told me about how she would go shopping for clothes against her family's budget and she would hide the clothes in her garage so that her husband wouldn't know. Another lady told me she secretly sneaks out to go send money to her relatives back in her country without her husband's knowledge.

A man told me how he takes out short term loans every week, gambles with that money at a casino and then pays the short term loan in "payments" so that his wife wouldn't find out about him gambling with their money. Another man also told me that he secretly pays his girlfriend's bills - obviously without his wife's knowledge.

A couple told me that they accidentally run into each other while they were both sneaking out to go pay off their "secretly obtained" loans. They had taken out the loans separately - for business they meant to hide from each other, only to run into each other at the loan office. I thought that was really funny because what are the odds of them taking out the loan from the same loan office? On a serious note though, that almost ended their marriage.

Another couple had constant marital stress because according to the wife, although her husband does have a stable income, she earns enough money to pay their bills and provide them with good financial stability, but all her husband does is spend money on big brand name items – specifically electronics and gadgets. She stated that her husband's outrageous spending is constantly rendering them broke all the time.

I could go on with many of these stories, but you get the gist. Finance is also vital in marriage.

As a matter of fact, money is a crucial cause of divorce in many marriages. Money can contribute to a happy home. But money can also destroy a happy home.

Allow me to elaborate; prior to the wedding, a couple had $7,000 (together). After planning the bride's "dream wedding" on paper, it appears they will end up spending about $17,000 total for the wedding - IF they don't modify the list. But the bride refuses to change anything; she wants the really big wedding she's been dreaming of since she was 10 years old - whether they can afford it or not. The groom is madly in love and so he agrees.

They end up borrowing the difference of $10,000 from somewhere. The wedding was beautiful and everyone is happy. Wedding is over and the guests leave to their various homes. After the wedding, real life does begin. The bills keep mounting up, including the $10,000 borrowed plus interest.

The lovely newlyweds begin to fight and blame each other every day. There is no happiness whatsoever. If God doesn't step in, they will end up in divorce court...because of MONEY.

What could they have done differently?

They could have modified the wedding list to make it more affordable. But they didn't.

And then there is the beautiful couple who have been married for a while and everything was peachy until the wife started earning more money than the hubby. Everything about her attitude begins to change. She no longer submits to her husband - because her income is now higher than his, suddenly he is beneath her.

You see where I'm going with this? Yep.

If God doesn't step in; they will also end up in divorce court...because of MONEY.

And there is the husband who was sweet and loving until he started earning a higher income than he's used to. He suddenly changes, if the wife is not lucky, she will even become his punching bag. Again, God is needed here too or divorce will set in. Please don't get me wrong. Money is good. But if we put God FIRST in the marriage, we will not get consumed by money.

Ecclesiastes 5:10 says,

"*Those who love money will never have enough. How meaningless to think that wealth brings true happiness*"

Hebrews 13:5 says, "*Don't love money; be satisfied with what you have. For God has said, "I will never fail you. I will never abandon you.*"

Let's remember that God created marriage as a permanent bond between a man and woman until death separates them. Don't allow money or anything else to separate your family.

Put God FIRST, family second, money and anything else LAST.

If you are married, may God bless your marriage.

If you are not married, may God bring you the RIGHT person.

Live within your means

There's an old saying that states;
"*Cut your coat according to your size*".
We must live within our means. Some women can single handedly destroy their marriage because they just can't bring themselves to be satisfied with what God has given them. They just HAVE to buy the most current "brand name" clothing and jewelry **every weekend** so that they can go partying with their friends.

They refuse to settle for any "no brand" items because they must compete with their friends.
As a result, they are always broke and struggling financially. Eventually, the husband gets fed up and divorces them.
Sadly, most of us are just like the woman I described above.

There's nothing wrong with pampering yourself if you can afford it. In fact, I am all for pampering yourself, but you must be able to comfortably afford it.
The logic is simple:
You can't spend what you don't have.
For example, you make $1,600 per month; your spouse makes $2,000 per month.
Together you guys bring home $3,600 per month in income.
You have two children.
That makes you a family of four.

Okay, let's break down the $3,600.00 income:

Monthly Rent/Mortgage= $1,400.00
Monthly Utilities= $350.00
Monthly Car Note= $550.00
Monthly Car Insurance= $250.00
Food for the family= $400.00
Telephone Bills= $150.00
Totaling $3,100.00

And that's just the basics. Other families have other bills in **addition** to the above. After paying all the bills above, you have a **balance of $500.00** Instead of putting the $500 in savings for a "rainy day", the wife decides she must buy the most beautiful Gucci bag she has ever seen. The bag will cost $2,990. But she just **has** to buy this bag at all cost.

So she fights her husband day and night for saying no to her request and she storms their bank account and clears their entire bank account, adds it to the $500 and purchases the Gucci handbag. Now her family is really broke and she is not even sorry for her actions.
It doesn't matter that her family will starve, she feels proud because her friends love her Gucci bag.

Luke 14:28 states,
"*But don't begin until you count the cost. For who would begin construction of a building without first calculating the cost to see if there is enough money to finish it?* "

Proverbs 21:20 wrote, "*The wise have wealth and luxury, but fools spend whatever they get.*"
Live within your means. Make your family your first priority. Don't spend more than you earn.

CHAPTER 4

Happily ever After

For your marriage to be *happily ever after*, you must obviously be happy. As I stated earlier, a true happy marriage consists of **true love, respect, honesty, loyalty, communication, transparency and the willingness to compromise**.
But for now, let's focus on **true love**.

1 Corinthians 13:4-7 says;
"Love is patient and kind. Love is not jealous or boastful or proud or rude. It does not demand its own way. It is not irritable, and it keeps no record of being wronged. It does not rejoice about injustice but rejoices whenever the truth wins out. Love never gives up, never loses faith, is always hopeful, and endures through every circumstance"

Your spouse must become your best friend and your most trusted confidant. **Speak up** when something goes wrong. Don't fake happiness when your heart is hurting or screaming for attention. Minimize the nagging though. If there's a problem, you two must sit and talk about it – maturely.

If you don't talk about it with your spouse and try to work out a solution, you will hold a grudge and grudges lead to bitterness, bitterness will lead to hatred, if harbored inside for a long time.

Besides, if you don't communicate what's in your heart, don't expect your spouse to know.
He or she is not a magician.
Another key factor to a happy marriage is **sex and lots of it.**

Most women (me included) have been guilty of using sex as "punishment" against our spouses when we get angry with them. Some of us wear jeans to bed and we place a padlock on it.
If you are still punishing your spouse with sex, be careful. We should never use sex as a weapon. This practice is dangerous and can drive your spouse into someone else's arms sooner or later. Bible says;
"Do not deprive each other of sexual relations, unless you both agree to refrain from sexual intimacy for a limited time so you can give yourselves more completely to prayer. Afterward, you should come together again so that Satan won't be able to tempt you because of your lack of self-control"- -- 1 Corinthians 7:5-6.

Don't be afraid or shy to try new things with your spouse. Invent your own stuff if you must.
If there's a certain sexual position you would love to try, by all means, open up to your spouse about it. 99% of the time, I guarantee you that your spouse would love to try any suggestions you bring on board. You and your spouse belong to each other and you guys obtained a legal license from God the day you said "I do" to each other. So don't be shy about it. Explore each other thoroughly.

Some men get suspicious when their woman suggests new things in the bedroom and they start wondering where their woman learned those new positions from. Yet they welcome such things from other women outside of their marriage. This limits many women and prevents them from being bold in the bedroom. But if you are a married woman, don't let that stop you from exploring your husband in the bedroom.

Scripture states in 1 Corinthians 7:3 that;
"The husband should fulfill his wife's sexual needs, and the wife should fulfill her husband's needs"

There is nothing wrong with trying new things with your spouse. No shame in that at all. Besides, if you do not try it with your spouse, chances are, you will end up trying it outside of your marriage.

If your spouse should make the mistake of cheating on you, you have a choice either to end the marriage or stay with that person - **if** you can get past the betrayal and trust them again. Although Jesus stated in Matthew 19:6,
"Since they are no longer two but one, let no one split apart what God has joined together"

If your spouse commits adultery, divorce is not a requirement, but it **is** permitted.
"But I say that a man who divorces his wife, unless she has been ***unfaithful****, causes her to commit adultery"* - Matthew 5:32
But if you decide to forgive and stay in the marriage, do not intentionally cheat on your spouse as a form on revenge. Do not keep revisiting the issue every time you have a misunderstanding. Forgiveness should mean forgiveness. Keep outsiders out of your marital issues. By telling people your business, you are making your family the topic of "town gossip" and disgracing yourself and your spouse. Don't make your marriage the topic of discussion.

Find different ways to spice up your marriage. Hang out together every chance you get and don't make every conversation about **the** kids.
Talk more like you did while dating. Role play if you both like that. Always think outside the box. It doesn't matter how long you've been married, together, you two can keep the romance alive. Start with the little things like complimenting on your spouse's clothes when they dress up, surprising them with flowers or lunch at work, randomly sending romantic texts - like how you are thinking about them, how much you are missing their presence, or a simple "I love you".

You know your spouse better than I do. You should know what their likes and dislikes are. If you don't know, find out and start doing them.

Even if you and your spouse have been estranged from each other for some time, you can still save the marriage - especially if you two are still living under the same roof. If you no one has moved on yet, it might not be too late.
If you are the offender, swallow your pride and apologize. Depending on the cause of the problem, "an apology" may not be enough. So your remorse must also reflect in your actions, followed by change.

Most importantly, ask for God's forgiveness and pray for God's intervention and direction.
As I stated above, when you both said "I do", you two became one. Be determined not to allow anything or anyone to come between you and your spouse.
Divorce has become popular because people give up too easily on their marriage.
People walk out of the marriage too quickly.

Don't give up easily.
Fight with prayer and do what is right for your family.

Bible says;
"Since they are no longer two but one, let no one split apart what God has joined together" - Mathew 19:6,

Another great wisdom you should learn to hold onto, is Ephesians 4:26-27'
"Don't sin by letting anger control you. Don't let the sun go down while you are still angry, for anger gives a foothold to the devil".

No matter how angry we get with each other, my husband and I always resolve the issue before we go to bed. If the issue can't completely be resolved in a day, we still find a way to get on what we call "common ground".

This practice has truly helped our marriage.
Yes marriage is very hard. Yes marriage isn't always "happily ever after". Yes you can't control your spouse' actions.

But you **can** keep God in your marriage, pray without ceasing. Pray TOGETHER.

1 Thessalonians 5:17 tells us to "*Never stop praying"*

A marriage should really begin with God and continue to keep God in it at all times.
If you didn't start your marriage **with** God, no problem, it's not too late.
You can **still invite** Him into your marriage.
Is happily ever after a possibility?
Oh yes. Absolutely!
Only God can make that possible though.
Make God the CENTER of your marriage.

PART 2

LIFE

CHAPTER 5

Abortion

Is abortion a good thing or a bad thing? I have heard this question many times and I believe it depends on who you ask. Years after my physically abusive relationship, I got into **another** relationship for about three years. It was a serious relationship. He proposed and I accepted and we got engaged. But a lot of things went wrong and I eventually broke it off with him. About one week after our break up, I realized I was carrying his baby. Yes. I was pregnant.

Our breakup was an ugly one. So I knew carrying his baby was the worst idea ever. And the thought of being a single mother scared me to death.
You can imagine my plight.
After contemplating on what to do for days, I made a decision to inform him about the pregnancy, although I wasn't really sure of what I wanted or expected from him – with regards to the pregnancy. After a few more days of contemplating, I paid him a visit and informed him that I was carrying his baby. I waited for his reaction to the news.

After a few minutes, he finally spoke and I guess he thought I was making it up, because he requested a visit to my doctor together for a pregnancy test. So we did, and the pregnancy was confirmed by the doctor – in his presence.
The doctor even did an ultrasound that day to show him. After we left the doctor's office, he said he will "get back to me".

Well, although he and I both lived in the States, and though he was a grown man in his twenties, he decided to consult with his mother - who was living in Ghana, about whether or not to take **responsibility** for the pregnancy.
And unfortunately for our unborn baby, his mother voted **negatively** against the pregnancy - because of some ongoing drama between her and my mother – in Ghana.
Apparently, my mother had been rude to his mother regarding something that he and I both knew absolutely nothing about.

And our unborn baby was the recipient of his mother's wrath against my mother.
Yep. A grown man needed his mother's approval before he could step up to his responsibilities.
Unfortunately, the father of my unborn child bailed on me because his mother needed retaliation on my mother. (*It is worth knowing that both mothers were in full support of our relationship in the beginning. In fact, they influenced the engagement greatly – initially, until they had a misunderstanding*)
Yes, I did not want to be a single mother and I didn't want to reconcile with my ex either, but I probably would have kept the baby if I had gotten some help from him or **anyone** at the time.
I was alone and broke. My life was completely shuttered. I was an emotional wreck.
I was so angry with myself for putting myself in that situation. I was confused as to why a grown man couldn't take a stand to be **responsible** for a child he had fathered.

I lived alone, my family had moved on with their own families, my parents had been divorced since I was a kid and they had both moved on with their own lives as well. No one cared whether I lived or died, except God – even though I didn't have a relationship with God at the time.
I was on an emotional roller-coaster. I couldn't sleep. I was depressed all the time. There was no way I could afford to raise a baby by myself.
I could barely make it on my own - financially.
I had a job, but I also had bills.

My ex fiancé had walked away from his responsibilities and I decided to leave him alone. After careful consideration of the pros and cons, after many tears, after many sleepless nights, I was emotionally and psychologically drained, broken, desperate, and angry with myself for "*mistaking a child for a man* "all these years.
I felt alone and stupid.
I finally made a very difficult decision to abort the baby - against my own personal beliefs on abortion. I visited **four** different doctors in an attempt to abort the pregnancy. The first three doctors refused to perform the abortion procedure because according to them, the pregnancy was 12 weeks too old. They even showed me an ultrasound of the baby inside me and it broke my heart to see my unborn child moving inside me, knowing I couldn't afford to keep it. Knowing I was about to kill it.
I convinced myself that I would be doing my baby a favor by aborting the pregnancy. So I quickly gathered myself emotionally and took my eyes off the ultra sound monitor. I begged them to perform the abortion for me.

But the first doctor said it was too risky due to the age of the pregnancy, he said I could die or I might not be able to bear children in the future. I didn't want to hear any of that. I didn't care about dying or the future. I left his office angry.
I went to two more doctors and it was the same story – they all said the same thing.
I visited a fourth doctor. The fourth doctor also told me the same thing. This time I didn't accept no for an answer. I begged him to help me. I cried to him for his help.

I even promised to sign a waiver showing that I was very much aware of the consequences and the risks. Once the waiver was signed, he finally obliged and yes, I aborted the pregnancy – thinking I'd be relieved once it was done.
Oh, it was the worst day of my life! I am not referring to the physical pain. That I could handle just fine. I was in so much emotional pain that I didn't even feel the physical pain. I felt awful!

You see, I thought the abortion would be the end of my problems. I thought I'd be free to easily move on with my life. Oh boy, I was dead wrong! It appears my problems were just beginning.
The emotional roller coaster got even worse.
I completely lost it. I cried more and more every night. I had nightmares every time I closed my eyes. One night, I got tired of crying and the emotional pain was too unbearable.
I got out of bed and started rummaging through my apartment to see what I could find to "end it all". I was actually contemplating suicide!

I didn't think anyone would notice my absence.
I figured after I die, my family will throw a big party; eat, drink and dance at my funeral party and move on with their lives the next day.
So I wouldn't be hurting anyone. I convinced myself that I'd be doing myself a favor if I commit suicide.
I was tired of the guilt and emotional pain caused by aborting my pregnancy. I had totally hit rock bottom.
I was broken; mind, soul and spirit. I was tired.

I finally found some pain killers inside my bathroom cabinet (Advil to be precise). I also found some roach killer, bathroom cleaners and decided to consume the whole bottle of pain killers in addition to the roach killer and bathroom cleaners and just die. I thought of mixing them all together. ***I was actually ready to commit suicide!!*** That was how badly I had regretted the abortion. But it was too late. I couldn't undo the abortion. I ***had to live*** with that choice I made - forever. I couldn't bear to live any longer.

But my **merciful** God saved my life that night and every night afterwards. Somehow, God changed my mind. God gave me strength.
God forgave me even though I hadn't yet asked for forgiveness. I put everything down and went back to my bedroom and after what seemed like an eternity, I finally fell asleep.
Now, let me tell you about the days, weeks, months and even years following the abortion. Oh my! I felt ***horrible*** in every sense of the word. I felt like I didn't deserve to live. I felt like I couldn't possibly "move on" with my life - like nothing happened. I felt like something huge had changed in my life. I felt like a murderer.
I cried endlessly every single night.

I had nightmares of the ultrasound image of my unborn child night after night. I would wake up every night following the nightmares and start crying all over again. This continued for many years, even after I got married to my husband, it still continued.

I needed to talk about it, so I told my husband about the abortion and I begged God for forgiveness over and over again.
Then, the nightmares finally stopped.
Psalm 51:17 says, "*The sacrifice you desire is a broken spirit. You will not reject a broken and repentant heart, O God*".

God forgave me and God allowed me to forgive myself. But looking back, I believe God forgave me even before the night I attempted suicide.
He saved my life that night because He had forgiven me already, He knew how broken and repentant my heart was, and He had more plans for my life. He wasn't done with me yet.
I wouldn't be writing this book if He had allowed me to die that night.
So if you ask me whether abortion is good or bad, based on **my** own personal experience, I will tell you without hesitation that abortion is most definitely NOT a good option.

Yes, I believed I wasn't in the right position to cater for a child by myself at the time and I also believed I was doing the right thing at the time. But I know now that I serve a LIVING God, who owns everything in this world and all I had to do was trust Him to cater for both myself and the child He was giving to me. I know now that I should have had that baby and kept him or her. If I had a time machine, I wouldn't have aborted the baby. If you are contemplating on abortion; I don't know what your situation is, and I don't know what you might be facing and feeling.

I don't know what your reasons are for even **considering** abortion as an option. But I do KNOW that I have once been where you are now.
And I will tell you that there is ***no reason*** under the sun to justify the abortion decision you are contemplating right now.
I guarantee you that, if you abort your unborn child, you will live to regret it for many years to come.

As hard as it may be, please turn the situation over to God. He is the only one who knows the end from the beginning. He is the only author and finisher of your faith.
He loves you and will direct your path.
There are many resources out there that you and your baby can benefit from. Feel free to contact me if you need help. I will do my best to help you.
But first allow God to direct your path. Go to Him in prayer.

Please understand that God doesn't make mistakes. He knew your situation prior to putting that baby inside you. God knows best.
Trust Him to step in and trust Him to take care of both you and the child. Trust Him to make a way where there is no way. Trust Him for great and mighty miracles. Please get on your knees right now and ask God for forgiveness. REPENT and ask God to take control of the wheel, because you simply cannot do this alone. It's a tough choice to make. Abortion is a decision that **will** change your life forever and **not** in a good way.
Ask God for strength, grace and wisdom.

Psalm 29:11 states, *"The LORD gives his people strength. The LORD blesses them with peace."*

John 14:27 says, "I am leaving you with a gift—peace of mind and heart. And the peace I give is a gift the world cannot give. So don't be troubled or afraid"
John 16:33, says "I have told you all this so that you may have peace in me. Here on earth you will have many trials and sorrows. But take heart, because I have overcome the world."

I pray that you will heed to my humble advice.
I have been there and I know what you are going through right now.
May God grant you STRENGTH and WISDOM to make the right decision.
May God help you if you are at that crucial place as you read this book.

Another Favorite Scripture

"And the Lord will be king over all the earth. On that day there will be one Lord—his name alone will be worshiped"

~ Zechariah 14:9-11 (NLT) ~

Chapter 6

On and Off

When I was a kid, my siblings nicknamed me "chameleon" because they said I had constant mood swings. According to them, I was nice and friendly only when I felt like it and I was very rude and unfriendly when I felt like it. Growing up, I would never go out of my way to start a fight, but I never "let go" if a person stepped on my toes ether. I was very confrontational and defensive.

I was also quick tempered, so we could be having a great time one minute and if something offends me the next second, by the time another minute arrives, I would be a totally different person – based on what or who caused the offense.
I would change very rapidly. ☺ I easily switch on and off very quickly. That's why I was nicknamed a chameleon. But thank God for His grace. God has brought me far.

Unfortunately, many Christians are "on again- off again" Christians. They are Christians based on the day of the week or the mood they are in at that moment. Some are "hard core Christians" if you catch them on their really good days.
On their bad days, well, they are just like any other unbeliever. They will show you no mercy should you step on their toes. You will see their "other side".
Some of them will ask you to wait while they "hang their Christian mask somewhere" so that they can fight you properly. ☺

My maternal grandmother was a very sweet lady, she always helped a lot of people, and she touched many lives positively. I don't recall ever seeing her argue, fight or confront anyone. She made sure to always avoid confrontation by "letting things go" - every time someone offended her.
She was the coolest person ever existed.
She minded her business. She never had any problems with anyone. No one had anything negative to say about her.

The only problem was that, she never went to church, she never worshiped God, she never prayed and she never worshiped Satan either. Spiritually speaking - she was neither hot nor cold. She was simply lukewarm. That's how she was raised. So she didn't really know God and she refused to worship Satan either. She didn't know the Lord.

Hebrews 10:26 says;
"***If we deliberately*** *continue sinning after we have received knowledge of the truth, there is no longer any sacrifice that will cover these sins*"

But if you consider yourself to be a Christian and yet you run a shift on serving God, you ought to know that being lukewarm is just as bad as worshipping "Baal" himself. Being lukewarm leaves you vulnerable to numerous spiritual attacks and those attacks get transferred to your marriage, your children and your family.

God cautions us against being "Lukewarm". Revelation 3:16 clearly says that;
"*Since you are like lukewarm water, neither hot nor cold, I will spit you out of my mouth*!"

Jesus said in Matthew 12:30 that;
"*Anyone who isn't with me opposes me, and anyone who isn't working with me is actually working against me*".

You cannot live your life being lukewarm.

You cannot be "in-between" and you cannot worship God part-time. You cannot worship God on "as needed basis". The medical term for "as needed" is "PRN". Please don't put your relationship with God on "PRN". You cannot worship God on YOUR terms or whenever YOU "*feel*" like. You must be a full time Christian at all times. You must keep all of God's decrees by putting them into practice. You must obey the word of God. You must fear God - that means doing everything right as if God were standing right in front of you – watching.
The fact is ***God is always watching***.

If you actively practice voodoo, if you are a fortune teller or psychic, if you are a "on again - off again" Christian, if you are a "lukewarm" Christian, if you are a double-minded Christian, (double-minded means today you are %100 Christian and come tomorrow, you are not so sure), If you are only a Christian on Sundays, or if you only get your "Christianity on" when you have an audience, you must be very, very careful because you are treading on a dangerous ground.
And that ground ***will*** sink soon or later. If you meet any of the above descriptions, Bible finds you guilty of committing "spiritual prostitution". Leviticus 20:6-8 says, "*I will also turn against those who commit spiritual prostitution by putting their trust in mediums or in those who consult the spirits of the dead. I will cut them off from the community. So set yourselves apart to be holy, for I am the LORD your God. Keep all my decrees by putting them into practice, for I am the LORD who makes you holy*".

In case you are not aware, let me be the first to inform you that God can and does see EVERYTHING we do. That means, while you can pretend to be something you are not before human beings, you cannot pretend with God.
Pretense will never fly with God. He is Supreme, He's All-Knowing, He's Omnipresent and He's Sovereign. He knows what you are going to do before you do it. Bible says He is a revealer of secrets. You cannot hide from Him.
So "faking it" and "duplication" will NOT work with God. God only accepts authenticity.
Be careful not to waver in your walk with Him.

Make a decision and stand by that decision – to worship God ONLY. But if you don't want to worship God, then move on to whatever you want to do. But you cannot do both. Simply be hot or cold, but never in between.

Family Differences

Every family has its ups and downs because even though everyone involved is family, they are all different individuals with different personalities. And when you put a group of people with various backgrounds and personalities, chaos does occur. So misunderstandings and differences of opinions in families are perfectly normal.
But we must all learn to resolve our differences quickly as a family. Learn to forgive each other genuinely as a family. Learn to keep friends and strangers out of our family matters. Spreading rumors about your own spouse to anyone who would listen and then turning around, sleeping with that same spouse, telling them how much you love them and flaunting that SAME spouse, makes both of you look stupid.
You will become a "laughing stock" as long as you remain married to the spouse you've been trashing. The folks you talked to, will mock and ridicule your marriage or family - all thanks to YOU. Some people might even tell your spouse the things you told them, creating more problems for your family. Remember, people will use whatever information you provide to them - to their own advantage - against your family. Your family should stand together and united no matter your differences.

Jesus stated in Matthew 12:25;
"*Any kingdom divided by civil war is doomed. A town or FAMILY SPLINTERED BY FEUDING WILL FALL APART*".

No family is problem-free. No family is perfect.
Just because it looks all rosy on the outside to onlookers doesn't mean its all perfect.
Just because their lawn looks greener than yours doesn't necessarily mean it is truly green.

Don't find out too late. Don't divide your family. Keep it together with fervent PRAYERS, so that Satan and his cohorts will not have a hole to slip through as a door to enter into your family.

This page was intentionally left blank

CHAPTER 7

God's Way

If you have read my book "***Spiritual Enrichment***", then you are aware that God gave me a job back in 2009 just before my husband lost his job. God kept me at that job for a little over six years. He fought for me day after day. There were times when I felt like I was walking on a thin ice at work. My job was threatened more times than I can count. There were many times at work, when I thought I would go crazy, because I got tired of being treated unfairly. **But God** held onto me and kept me strong and sane. He never let go.

God never left me. It didn't matter how high expectations or goals were set for me - God **always exceeded** them. God constantly baffled my mind. God KEPT me at that job and God made me **invincible and untouchable** to all those people who were after my job. God made sure that no one could touch me. As King David would say, He made me as surefooted as the deer.

Then one day the company decided to close down **permanently**. **Everyone**, from the big bosses to the little people, was laid off - including me. I was confused. I didn't understand God. A million questions started flooding through my head. Questions like "why would God allow this to happen now?" "Why can't I catch a simple break?" I knew this lay off could only happen with God's approval. Remember, He gave me that job.
He alone had the power to take it away from me. And to me, the layoff happened at the worst possible time.

I found myself questioning God again;
"Why would God keep and protect my job for six years and then choose this worst time possible to take it away?" "Why would God take us back to square one?
I knew better than to question my God. I knew Isaiah 55:8-10 tells me that "His ways are higher than our ways and His thoughts are higher than our thoughts".
But I was so devastated that I couldn't help, but question Him. I had many questions. I just didn't get it.

In the middle of my questions, I remembered Abraham and Sarah. I remembered Abraham was 100 years old and Sarah was 90 years old when their son Isaac was born.
100 years old! And 90 years old!
Abraham and Sarah waited **that** long to be blessed with **a son.** They didn't even think they would get to be parents until God intervened. Just like I didn't think I'd get that job at the time God gave it to me. And when God finally gave Abraham and Sarah a child, all of a sudden, God asked Abraham to sacrifice the baby's life for Him in Genesis 22.

Can you just imagine what Abraham and Sarah must have gone through with God's request?
I am sure Abraham didn't quite understand why God would make such a request.
I mean, Isaac was his ONLY child, and he knew there was no way he and Sarah could have another child without God's intervention.
But he also **knew** God GAVE him that child in the first place, so he trusted that God **can** give him another child if he obeyed God and sacrificed Isaac as God had requested. **He trusted that God knew what He was doing.**

I reminded myself that Abraham obeyed God's instructions. But he later realized that God was just testing him to see whether he truly feared God. History has it; Abraham passed the test with flying colors. I realized that **this** was **my** test and sadly, I was failing that test miserably.

Instead of me trusting God, I was trying to understand why God would allow this to happen to me. I was worried about the future even though I knew God was with me. I had failed the test. I begged God for forgiveness.
The story of Abraham and Sarah got me thinking. It made me more confident that, for God to finally take my job away, He must have something better planned for me. Greater things are underway. Sometimes God does things that we can't comprehend. Things happen in our lives that our human minds can't fathom no matter how hard we try.
Bible says;
"***God's way is perfect. All the Lord's promises prove true.*** *He is a shield for all who look to him for protection*" - Psalm 18:30.

If you don't understand what God is doing in your life or if you don't understand why God allows certain things to happen to you, as Stephen would say "just trust Him". We are still alive because God still has greater things planned for us. Try not to question Him. Just know that His ways are PERFECT. Isaiah 55:8-10 says; "***My thoughts are nothing like your thoughts," says the Lord. And my ways are far beyond anything you could imagine. For just as the heavens are higher than the earth, so my ways are higher than your ways and my thoughts higher than your thoughts. The rain and snow come down from the Heavens and stay on the ground to waste the earth. They cause the grain to grow, producing seed for the farmer and bread for the hungry***"

What's yours is yours

If you find yourself having to constantly fight for something, that thing probably isn't yours to begin with. If you are always fighting over your partner, that person isn't yours. If you are constantly heartbroken over a person and if that person only shows you respect and love in their time of need – you should consult with God for direction - you might be wasting your time. They are using you. True love should flow easily and naturally without any struggle. True love should only GROW over time and not reduce over time. Keep in mind that no one can take what God has instituted for you. And you cannot take what God has instituted for someone else.
Instead of trying so hard to hold onto what may belong to another person - LET IT GO.

There's no such thing as "accidentally letting go", because, even if you "accidentally let go" of something that is meant for you - God WILL bring it back to you. But if you keep trying to forcibly hold onto someone or something, it doesn't matter how long you keep them - you WILL eventually lose. You will be fighting a losing battle. Let go!

John 10:29 says,

"*For my Father has given them to me, and he is more powerful than anyone else. No one can snatch them from the Father's hand*".

Ephesians 1:11-11 says,

"*Furthermore, because we are united with Christ, we have received an inheritance from God, for he chose us in advance, and HE MAKES EVERYTHING WORK OUT ACCORDING to HIS PLAN*"

NO ONE can take what God has given to you. Instead of forcing to keep what belongs to another person - LET IT GO and PRAY to God to bring what belongs to YOU. Don't chase after someone else's husband or wife, even if they leave their spouse to be with you, they will end up leaving you for someone else, because they were never yours in the first place. Don't keep taking what doesn't belong to you.

Life is too short - Don't waste your years on someone or something that will eventually leave you anyway.
Ask God to give you your own.

Fighting God's Way

I remember God revealing the true heart of a friend towards me, God made me see what my friend truly thought of me. I was shattered and surprised, so hurt that instead of allowing God to take care of His own revelation, I stupidly confronted that person. I took matters into my own hands. That has always been my problem; waiting for God to act.
Most of us are just like that. We tend to fight spiritual battles in the flesh. We forget that we cannot physically fight a spiritual battle. You will lose. It's that simple.

Bible has said in Ephesians 6:12 that;
" *We are not fighting against flesh and blood enemies, but against evil rulers and authorities of the unseen world, against mighty powers in this dark world, and against evil spirits in the heavenly places*".

That means instead of going to fist fight or argue with whoever you think may be destroying or fighting you spiritually, you should pray and let the Holy Spirit do the fighting for you. Pray on your knees, standing up, sitting down, jumping or walking, yelling, shouting, screaming - it doesn't matter how you do it - just PRAY.

That fight is God's fight. Not yours. Don't try to fight battles that only God can win. If you do, you might not live to regret it.

Just the right time

There was an elite program that I wanted badly to be accepted for. The program only offered ONE opportunity to apply and be accepted. That means if you miss that ONE opportunity or if you get denied, you miss that one chance and there are no second chances - that's IT. So when my ONE chance came, I prayed for God's approval before I applied for the program. Shortly after I applied, I received an email invitation for a digital interview. The email explained that a digital interview means I will be interviewed by an individual live via webcam. I had never done a digital interview before. I love technology, but I am still "old school" and would have preferred a face to face interview. I felt it would be much easier for me to build a rapport with the interviewer if we met face to face than over a camcorder. I was nervous.

My first thought was to practice doing a digital interview by role playing with my computer's webcam. After all the role playing and practicing, when the time came for my digital interview, instead of one interviewer, there were two ladies ready to interview me via webcam and wouldn't you know it; I FROZE. When I finally gathered the courage to speak, I completely failed the interview. For some reason, I couldn't bring myself to be "comfortable" with this new way of interviewing. I kept wondering "whatever happened to good old fashioned face to face interview?" ☺

After about five minutes into the very awkward digital interview, one of the ladies said they will get back to me. I knew what that meant and sure enough by the next day I received an email from them saying, sorry they had decided to pursue other candidates. I thought I had blown my ONE chance. But then God gave me another chance by offering me another digital interview with the same program and the same company.
I don't know why I was so scared of the mere mention of "digital interview ".
Yes. I blew that opportunity too.
And before you ask; YES. REALLY! ☺

I was convinced that there was no way I would get another chance. I thought my opportunity was over. But then weeks later, I received an email asking me whether I was still interested in the program and I answered yes. Then they scheduled another digital interview with me. I couldn't believe it! I had been given a THIRD chance!!!
I thought: "This is definitely from a favor from God!"

So I had a "heart to heart" conversation with God about the program. This time, by God's grace, I aced the digital interview. I was surprisingly comfortable, calm and collected with the interview this time. When the interview was over, the interviewer accepted me into the program instantly, but I had to meet with one of their agents in order to complete the process of acceptance.

I was to take some very important items the agent needed in order to complete the acceptance process.
Well, when I met with the agent, I didn't have the items I was supposed to give to the agent, because I had taken the wrong items. There was no way I could return home for those items. While waiting for the agent to see me, I kept praying to God for His intervention in the matter. Low and behold; God granted me favor with the agent.

Isaiah 49:8-9 says;
"*At just the right time, I will respond to you.*
On the day of salvation I will help you.
Christ came at just the right time!
I trusted that God will keep His promise and I left it all alone. But God showed up at JUST THE RIGHT TIME!"

Worth noting

Just because you have repented of your old ways and just because you are a now a new creation in Jesus Christ - doesn't mean that life will be a "breeze" for you. Just because you are living a holy and righteous life as required by Yahweh, doesn't mean everything in your life will go smoothly all the time.

You WILL face many hardships and many obstacles, trials, tribulations - your faith will be tested greatly in more ways than one. But I want to remind you that God had already predicted your current state - before you were born.

Remember that God's WORD IS FAITHFUL! If you are genuinely FOR Him, if you are genuinely SERVING God, then KNOW that God IS also FOR YOU. He WILL protect YOU. He will provide for you.

Bible says in Psalm 34:19-20 that, "*The righteous person faces many troubles, but the Lord comes to the rescue each time. For the Lord protects the bones of the righteous; not one of them is broken!*"

God's Resume`

The devil has a way of trying to deter the progress of God's children. Notice I used the word "TRYING", because if you belong to God, all Satan can do to you - is "TRY". He WILL fail – but even Satan doesn't give up - he'll keep trying. When that happens, we MUST remind ourselves to ONLY SEE what God has promised us in His WORD. We must ask God to constantly remind us of HIS faithfulness in our lives.
We must consciously review God's resume in our lives in order for us to keep moving forward.

One night after praying, I went on Facebook briefly and came across this on a friend's status: "*Lord, I know what things look like, I know what I see, but I care more about what you told me, not what I see, Lord, I still trust you*".

Powerful. Isn't it? Just powerful! I was moved because I can relate in every sense of the word. Really - we can ALL relate. I was also moved by her words and the strong faith she exhibited - despite whatever she might be going through. You see, this lady KNOWS the miracles God is capable of performing. She KNOWS God doesn't lie. She KNOWS God is faithful and all God's promises are true.
Although things aren't looking "hopeful", she has made a decision to ONLY SEE what God has promised to do in her life - through His WORD. Simply powerful!

I don't know what her situation is, but I know that, just as Jesus said to the woman with the issue of blood in Mark 5:34;
"*Daughter, your faith has made you well. Go in peace. Your suffering is over.*"
Jesus is saying the very same thing to this lady and to those of us who STILL believe in God.
My friend, no matter how useless and hopeless your situation is, no matter what you are experiencing, don't look at the hopelessness of your situation. Don't look at the impossibility of your situation. I KNOW it's a difficult thing to do, but focus on what God has told YOU in HIS WORD. I need you to tell yourself that (and BELIEVE) that;
"I KNOW the Lord is always with me.
I will not be shaken, for he is right beside me"
.. Psalm 16:8.

Bible says the earnest prayer of a righteous person has great power and produces wonderful results..,,,,(James 5:16)

But that doesn't mean as soon as you pray, boom - ta-da, your prayers are answered.
It means, in ADDITION to the prayer, you MUST acknowledge that God is faithful and WILL not let you down.
How do you know? YOU JUST KNOW!..
FAITH is when "YOU JUST KNOW!"

I want YOU to "JUST KNOW" - that whatever you prayed for has been answered.

Let's sing a song of David in psalm 30;

"*I will exalt you, Lord, for you rescued me. You refused to let my enemies triumph over me. O Lord my God, I cried to you for help, and you restored my health. You brought me up from the grave, O Lord. You kept me from falling into the pit of death. Sing to the Lord, all you godly ones! Praise his holy name. For his anger lasts only a moment, but his favor lasts a lifetime! Weeping may last through the night, but joy comes with the morning. When I was prosperous, I said, "Nothing can stop me now!" Your favor, O Lord, made me as secure as a mountain. Then you turned away from me, and I was shattered. I cried out to you, O Lord. I begged the Lord for mercy, saying, "What will you gain if I die, if I sink into the grave? Can my dust praise you? Can it tell of your faithfulness? Hear me, Lord, and have mercy on me. Help me, O Lord. You have turned my mourning into joyful dancing. You have taken away my clothes of mourning and clothed me with joy, that I might sing praises to you and not be silent. O Lord my God, I will give you thanks forever!*"

Amen!!

This page was intentionally left blank

God, Is this really from you?

Sometimes we pray for something and God grants our request. We get excited. We are very grateful to God for His provision. But then everything God gave us - suddenly feels threatened. We see every answer God granted to us - suddenly crumpling down. We get confused. We ask ourselves;
"Wait a minute - God GAVE ME this thing, so why am I losing it?" "I prayed - so why are things going wrong?"
And you begin to wonder; "Did God really give me this thing?", or "Is God even real?" or "Does God truly answer prayers?"
Question after question begin to flood through your mind and you get confused. It just doesn't make sense!

My dear friend, if YOU are experiencing any of the above scenarios, then God wants you to know that; He - GOD - causes "EVERYTHING to work together for the good of those who love Him and are called according to his purpose for them"... (Romans 8:28)

God NEEDS YOU to UNDERSTAND that,
From eternity to eternity He IS God.
Therefore, absolutely NO ONE can snatch anyone out of His hand and NO ONE can undo what God has done in YOUR life. So while it may SEEM as if you are about to lose everything God GAVE to YOU, God is asking you to ONLY SEE AND TRUST HIM.

God is talking to YOU right now in Isaiah 44:21. He says, "*Pay attention, O Naomi, O Paul, O Mary, O Rose, O Kenneth, O Laura, O Phil, O Beatrice, O Nathaniel, O Eva..... (PUT YOUR NAME THERE), for YOU are my servant, O Naomi.. (PUT YOUR NAME THERE). I, the Lord, made you, and I will NOT forget YOU*"

God IS **STILL** in control my dear. So quit expecting your breakthrough to come from people, stones or rocks and simply TRUST Jehovah Jireh. As a friend of mine puts it, "What's the alternative to God?"...NONE.
He IS the ONLY way. Confidently trust Him.

There comes a time in our lives when God allows Satan to put our faith to test. He wants to see just how much we love and trust Him. He wants to see whether we will still hold onto our faith in God when the going gets tough. God allowed Satan to test Job in Job 1:12. And as we all know, Satan took away everything Job owned including his health. But Job's faith never wavered. Job stood firm in the Lord. If you read the entire book of Job, you will find that it wasn't easy for Job.
There were days he cried and there were days he questioned God.

But Job NEVER gave up. He trusted God. He knew Satan couldn't possibly touch him without God's approval and he also knew God was faithful.

Let's not forget my friend Simon Peter;
Jesus told Peter in Luke 22:31-32, "*Simon, Simon, Satan has asked to sift each of you like wheat. But I have pleaded in PRAYER for you, Simon that your FAITH should NOT fail*".

My dear friend, I don't know just how deep Satan has you sinking, but I want you to hold on to your FAITH in God. Don't forget that God's Word will always do what He has sent it to do in your life.

It's okay to cry and its okay to question God, but don't ever give up. Trust God.
Remember God's faithfulness in your life.
Remember God's resume over the years.
If you hang on long enough, God WILL give you a testimony. Be sure to share that testimony when it comes.

Keep on asking

I remember sometime ago I had prayed for something and I didn't get it right away, I was disappointed and angry with God to the extent of deciding not to ever pray again.
Today, I look back and I ask myself; "REALLY Naomi?"
If we get angry and impatient with God, do you really think He cares? Do you think that will influence God to "speed" things up for you? Really? Nope. I think not!
Don't get tired of praying for something.
Don't get impatient with God. I know it's hard.

But don't give up.

As Mathew 7:7-11 states,

"*KEEP ON ASKING*"*"Keep on asking, and you will receive what you ask for. Keep on seeking, and you will find. Keep on knocking, and the door will be opened to you. For everyone who asks, receives. Everyone who seeks, finds. And to everyone who knocks, the door will be opened. You parents—if your children ask for a loaf of bread, do you give them a stone instead? Or if they ask for a fish, do you give them a snake? Of course not! So if you sinful people know how to give good gifts to your children, how much more will your heavenly Father give good gifts to those who ask him*"

Acknowledging Red Flags

When I ponder over my life and I reminisce on all my past mistakes and all the wrong choices I have made in my life, I realize that God gave me many red flags in every stage of my life and in every situation I ever encountered. But I ignored all the signals from God, both intentionally and unintentionally. I realize that instead of following God's lead, I took my own path.

I have come to realize that God looks out for every single one of us - even the ones that don't really know Him. God stated in Isaiah 45:4 that,
"*I have even called you by your name; I have named you, THOUGH YOU HAVE NOT KNOWN ME*".
Bible says He made all of us and He will not forget us. God is determined to order the steps of His children. But He is also FAIR to all His children. That's why He protects us from those who mean us harm. He directs you.
Sometimes, certain things happen that causes us to wonder and to question ourselves;
"HOW did I not see this coming?" OR
"HOW did I get here?".....
Oh, but YOU DID see it coming!
You just CHOSE to ignore it.
If you think back over the years, you will realize that God SHOWED YOU ALL the "RED FLAGS" in that situation or with that person - you are dealing with today" but you CHOSE not to identify those "red flags".

If you think back, you will realize that God WAS WITH YOU every step of the way - GIVING YOU ALL the pointers to the "red flags" and you CHOSE to ignore His direction and you CHOSE to pursue your own desire....
So you see? YOU DID see it coming!

Yes. God ALWAYS leads us. But most of us don't recognize God's voice when we hear it and we don't recognize His hands when we see it.
Some of us also intentionally ignore God's direction in order to take our own path - hence creating messes and regrets in our lives.

When you are not sure whether or not the "red flags" are truly from God, God tells you in Jeremiah 33:3 to "*Ask me and I will tell you remarkable secrets you do not know about things to come*"
Don't ignore red flags. Pray about them!

Commit all your plans to God and "*Seek HIS WILL in ALL you do, and he will show you which path to take*"...Proverbs 3:6.

This will save you a whole lot of headaches and regrets in the future.

CHAPTER 8

Being a Christian

A Muslim friend of mine once said to me;

"We Muslims are more "Christians" than you Christians".

I thought that statement he made was funny because he and every Muslim do not believe in Jesus Christ as Lord. Acts 11:26 tells us that "***It was at Antioch that the believers were first called Christians***" because their behavior, activity, and speech were **like** Jesus Christ.

The word "Christian" means, that person has a relationship with Jesus Christ and that person truly belongs to Jesus Christ. According to the media, a strong Pastor n Chicago, one of my favorite gospel singers, is alleged to have had "an adulterous 8 year affair with his former Church secretary".

This story broke my heart because I thought highly of him. And I know a lot of people were hurt by this news, because almost everyone threw judgments at him. We must remember that he is human and we humans have the tendency to make stupid decisions and silly mistakes.
There's no doubt that what he did was wrong in the sight of God and man, not to mention his wife. But keep in mind that this man is a fallen saint and keep in mind that it could have been you. Yours might not be an adulterous affair, but I bet yours is equally horrific. You just haven't been caught - yet. So "cool it" with the judgments.

God said in Romans 12:19 "Vengeance is mine". Only God is allowed to judge.
As Christians, when a fellow saint falls, it is our responsibility to help them find their way back to God. It is okay to rebuke them for a minute, but no judgments. Kicking someone who is already down is not the way of God. When a fellow servant of God falls, they are obviously spiritually dead and it is our responsibility to help them LIVE again.
Ezekiel 16:6-7 says;
"But I came by and saw you there, helplessly kicking about in your own blood. As you lay there, I said, 'Live!"
When a person falls spiritually, Satan throws a party. It is our responsibility to disappoint Satan, by helping that person find their way back to God. Please don't step all over a person who is already down. Help them get up and live again.
God will greatly reward you.

Letting Go

Being a Christian begins with repentance of sins, and then having a true and genuine relationship with Jesus Christ. Being a Christian is a way of life. It means studying the WORD of God and applying every word of wisdom in the WORD to your daily life. Being a Christian is LIVING the WORD of God.
Bible says in Matthew 7:13-14 that;
"*You can enter God's Kingdom only through the narrow gate. The highway to hell is broad, and its gate is wide for the many who choose that way. But the gateway to life is very narrow and the road is difficult, and only a few ever find it*".

The only way to enter the Kingdom of God is by being doers of the WORD. The only way to enter God's kingdom is through our Lord and Savior Jesus Christ. One cannot perceive to be a Christian without having a true and personal relationship with Jesus Christ our Lord.

There was a time in my life when someone made me very angry and deeply hurt.
After about one week, I realized that being angry was beginning to hurt me more than that person, because every time I thought about what they did to me, my heart would beat furiously.
I realized that the anger was eating me up and blocking many blessings for me.
I found that I could no longer feel the presence of God in my life.

I realized that being angry was gradually standing between me and my God. I realized I needed to **forgive** my offender.
But I knew there's no way I could do it alone because I was deeply hurt. I knew I needed the power of the Spirit and the grace of God to help me. I committed the matter to God. I asked God to fight the battle for me. I begged God to uproot all the anger, malice and the urge to avenge - out of my heart. I asked God to fill my heart with a **spirit of forgiveness** and fruit of the Spirit and he granted my request. I forgave and moved on.

Anger is toxic and dangerous for everyone, especially Christians. Think about it, when you get angry, you cease to be happy and the longer you drag it, the more threatening it becomes for your health. So anger is bad even for unbelievers. Although it's perfectly okay to be angry, Bible specifically warns us not to sin by letting anger control us. Don't allow anger to take root and a life of its own in your heart. Cain was so angry with God and Abel that he actually killed his innocent brother!
Saul wanted to kill David so badly because he was very angry with him for the awesome things God was doing through David. Saul's anger for David was so strong that he transferred that anger to his own son Jonathan.
Though Saul's love for his son Jonathan was strong, his hatred and anger for David was even stronger. Anger ultimately destroyed him.
You see, Forgiveness is hard. No doubt.

Forgiving someone can be very difficult. Forgiveness is a gigantic move. To truly forgive someone from the bottom of your heart **requires the GRACE of God**. No one can do it alone.
But living a Christian life is harder. Living a "Christ-like" life is not easy. Living a holy life - pleasing and acceptable to God is never a "bed of roses or an easy road".
Listen, as long as you consider yourself to be **a Christian**, you must forgive your offenders just as God our father has forgiven your many sins.
Forgiveness is really not for the person who hurt you. Forgiveness is for you.

Forgiveness is good for **your** health, **your** spiritual growth and **your** blessings and **your** salvation.
Forgiveness is not an option for us – Christians.
Our God is love and as hard as it may seem, we must love even the "not so easy to love" people in our lives.
By refusing to forgive and holding onto anger and malice, you are freely giving the other person the key to your life and happiness.
Anger destroys your relationship to God.
You might say, "But they don't deserve my forgiveness after what they did to me"
Well, let me ask you a question:
Do you deserve God's love and forgiveness for your sins?

When we pray "The Lord's prayer" in Mathew 6:9-13, we say;
"*And **forgive** us **our trespasses** as we **forgive** those who trespass against us.*"

We are asking God to **forgive** us in the same way we also forgive those who hurt us.
You must forgive even if they are not sorry.
Please don't allow bitterness and anger to separate you from God.
Apostle Paul wrote in Romans 8:38-39;
"*And I am convinced that nothing can ever separate us from God's love. Neither death nor life, neither angels nor demons, neither our fears for today nor our worries about tomorrow—not even the powers of hell can separate us from God's love. No power in the sky above or in the earth below—indeed, nothing in all creation will ever be able to separate us from the love of God that is revealed in Christ Jesus our Lord*"

When we are hurt and angry, Forgiveness becomes very hard and incomprehensible.
You can offend someone in 1990 come 2016, they are still angry with you, waiting for the opportunity to retaliate.
Some people can be angry forever, and wonder why God hasn't been answering their prayers.
Some people will say "*I can never forgive you for what you did to me*"
Proverbs 20:22 tells us not to say, *"I will get even for this wrong"*. It says to wait for the Lord to handle the matter.
Bible tells us that vengeance is the Lord's.
It doesn't matter what we've done, when we return to God He forgives us. So **who are we** to hold grudges? How can you possibly call yourself a servant of God, a Christian and hold grudges and bitterness in your heart against your neighbor?

That person has already hurt you badly; don't give them the pleasure of controlling your destiny by refusing to forgive them. Yes. If you don't forgive them, you have literally handed them the key to your salvation and your destiny. The **anger you feel towards them will eventually grow into bitterness and bitterness** can and will destroy you - if you don't let go.
Bitterness will grow into darkness within your heart and when that happens, believe me when I tell you, that God WILL leave your heart and soul. Beloved, God is LIGHT and be rest assured that He will NOT reside in darkness.

Yes He said he will never leave you nor forsake you, but if you fill your heart with darkness, you are not welcoming Him anymore, you are asking Him to leave and He will oblige to your unspoken request. Imagine Satan having a beautiful field day the day God exits your life.

Jesus said in John 8:12 that, "*I am the **light** of the world. If you follow me, you won't have to walk in darkness, because you will have the light that leads to life.*"

If you are a Christian, Forgiveness is mandatory. It's nonnegotiable. It's a must!
If you want to feel God's presence in your life, you must forgive.
Bible says, if you forgive those who sin against you, God will also forgive you.
But if you refuse to forgive others, God will not forgive your sins.

My friends, before you entertain anger, bitterness, grudge and hatred, before you entertain revenge and un-forgiveness;

Ask yourself these questions;
Is this person worth my health?
Is this person worth my happiness?
Is this person worth my life?
Is this person worth my blessings?
Is this person worth my relationship with God?
Is this person worth my salvation?

If you answered "NO" to these questions, then you better get on your knees and pray like you've never prayed before.
Ask God to cleanse your heart of all anger, bitterness and darkness.
Ask God to fill your heart with His light and the Spirit of forgiveness.
Ask God to grant you the grace you need to forgive **and let go**.

Sin is easy

It's so easy for us to fight someone who offends us. It's hard to forgive someone who has treated us unfairly. It's so easy to be angry with someone for so long for "*whatever*" they did. It's easy for us to take vengeance for a wrong done to us.
It's so easy to fornicate. It's so easy to commit adultery. It's easy to cheat and steal what does not belong to us. It's so easy to hold grudges and hate someone. The pleasures of sin are many and easily attained. For some of us, it's easy to commit murder or rape. For example, terrorists are committed to killing and they actually take pleasure in killing themselves along with thousands of innocent people.

Sad thing is, they have convinced themselves that they are doing it all for the glory of God - when God has absolutely nothing to do with it.
It's easy to justify our sinful actions. Choosing to do the wrong thing is easier than doing the right thing. Sin is super easy and super fun.
But sin has great consequences.

Bible says in Romans 6:23,
"*For the wages of sin is death, but the free gift of God is eternal life through Christ Jesus our Lord*".

We sin easily without thinking about the consequences because it's always the easy way out. We easily tell lies because lying is way easier than telling the truth.

A very wise and powerful man of God puts it this way; "*Sin is like jumping from a very tall building and enjoying the ride until you hit the floor and go oops*".
When the consequences of sin hit home, sin is suddenly not so fun after all.
Regrets begin to set in, followed by "had-I-known".
True Christianity is extremely hard.
I am not talking about ***religion***, because being "religious" is easy too. Anyone can do it. Anyone can go around bombing innocent people because they have been led to believe that's "God's will".

Anyone can fake a religious personality and yet be their true self behind closed doors. Anyone can follow a bunch of religious "dos and don'ts".
Jesus talked about the Pharisees who were great at practicing religion rather than practicing His word. Mathew 23:1-7 reads;
"Then Jesus said to the crowds and to his disciples, The teachers of religious law and the Pharisees are the official interpreters of the law of Moses. So practice and obey whatever they tell you, but don't follow their example. For they don't practice what they teach. They crush people with unbearable religious demands and never lift a finger to ease the burden. Everything they do is for show. On their arms they wear extra wide prayer boxes with Scripture verses inside, and they wear robes with extra long tassels. And they love to sit at the head table at banquets and in the seats of honor in the synagogues. They love to receive respectful greetings as they walk in the marketplaces, and to be called 'Rabbi"

That's religion and that's **not** what I am referring to. **I'm talking about walking with God, living the word, breathing the word and exhibiting the word**. I'm talking about letting the light of God shine through you. I'm talking about a total stranger seeing God in you without you uttering a word. I'm talking about forgiveness, loving everyone in spite of how they treat you, obedience, honesty, integrity, humility and everything the bible talks about.

For most of us, the hardest thing to do is to **walk away** from a fight or an argument. Some of us can not rest until we have retaliated. I know, because I used to be just like that. I used to love retaliation.

I remember how in the past, I would decide to forgive someone for something they had done to me, but the devil constantly gave me all the reasons why I should go retaliate. And Satan eventually won in those days. But thanks be to God, Satan has lost that battle now.
Satan no longer has that hold on me.

The other day, I saw a clip floating around on social media about two women fighting in the street in traffic and as I watched them go at each other yelling and screaming, I saw my "old-self" in them and I thought;

"Oh my God, so that's how silly, stupid and foolish I also looked back in the day when I used to fight and argue!" ☺

I told myself I will never put myself in that situation ever again. I thanked God for opening my eyes. He has brought me far. I'm grateful. The truth is that most people resort to sin because it's easier, and worshiping God truthfully and spiritually is truly the most difficult thing to do. But once you get used to it, you will find that serving the Lord is the SWEETEST THING EVER.

That is why you see many Christians backsliding. That's why you see many fake Pastors and Prophets. It's very difficult when we try to walk with God in the flesh and by our own might. We all need to seek Spiritual Insight and wisdom from the Lord to help us walk with God genuinely - in truth and in Spirit. Bible tells us that God is spirit and the only way to worship Him is **in spirit and in truth**.

It's hard to be a genuine Christian and so many Christians don't always make it.
Matthew 7:13-14 says,

"You can enter God's Kingdom only through the ***narrow*** *gate. The highway to hell is broad, and its gate is wide for the many who choose that way. But the gateway to life is very narrow and the road is difficult, and only a few ever find it*".

The songwriter says; "***Lord, to give up, I'd be a fool***". I am in 100% agreement with that song because the God I serve is a God of multiplication and not subtraction or division. He is a God of increase and not decrease. He is a God of **forward ever, backwards never**.

Tell yourself; "My God has made me surefooted as the dear, not weak and loose footed". If you have been truly serving God and if you have truly and genuinely repented of your old ways, be rest assured that God has planted your feet on a solid rock and if you stay with Him, nothing can topple you down. I know from personal experience that Satan tries to send you back to your old ways when he sees how far God has brought you in the Spirit. Satan starts infiltrating your mind and dreams with sins from your past, when he sees where God is taking you. First he will remind you of how horrible you did in your past and he will tell you that God will never forgive you (even though God forgave you the very minute you repented and gave your life to Him).

And if that doesn't work, Satan will constantly remind you of "the pleasures" of your sins from the past and he will begin to convince you to go back to that life. You must understand that Satan isn't very happy about losing your soul. In fact, he is angry about losing the soul he originally **thought** he had – **your soul**. Satan will do **anything** to get your soul **back** to him. You must not give in.

And please know that you cannot fight and defeat the devil alone. You simply don't have that kind of power on your own. **You must get help from the Lord through prayer.** You must pray continually and ask God to keep your feet on that solid rock, where He has placed you. Then, begin to think over your life, think about where God has brought you from and though you have no idea where God is taking you, you will realize that it's not worth going back to your old ways.

Don't give up even if you are spiritually not where you ought to be yet. Let prayer remain your best weapon. Seek Spiritual wisdom and insight from the Lord. Ask God to keep you in His light and under His wings and never let you go.
Ask God to keep you under His safe haven where your sinful ways cannot reach you. Ask God to continue to keep you strong in His spirit.

Remember, God will not keep you strong if you don't want to be strong - because He has given us the freedom and the freewill to make our own choices. You made a decision to repent and to accept Jesus Christ as your Lord and Savior and you must make that same decision to stick to Him and never let go. You must seek God's help and guidance to keep you strong from falling into Satan's trap.
Romans 12:10-13 shows us what the "marks of a true Christian should be.
It says; *"Love each other with genuine affection, and take delight in honoring each other. Never be lazy, but work hard and serve the Lord enthusiastically. Rejoice in our confident hope. Be patient in trouble, and keep on praying. When God's people are in need, be ready to help them. Always be eager to practice hospitality."*

Being a true Christian is a difficult life to live. But I guarantee you that if you walk on that very **narrow** route, you will never regret it.
It will be the best decision you will ever make.
Remain vigilant in the Lord.
Don't allow the devil in.

Duty of a Christian

I took a stroll the other day and decided to buy eggs from Kroger. You know how it is - we go to the store with the intention of buying ONE thing and you end up leaving the store with TEN things. Well, I left Kroger with a lot more than originally intended - with total disregard of the fact that I didn't drive there. I had many shopping bags in both hands. I think it's safe to say that I was indeed struggling with all those heavy bags.

I immediately began to regret my decision to buy more than I had planned. As I crossed the street, a school bus dropped off a few high school kids in front of the subdivision and the kids started walking to their various homes. Suddenly, one of the white girls walked back to me and said "Hi Ma'am, can I help you with the bags? I see you are struggling".

I was shocked because people don't do that anymore. People don't help strangers anymore - for many different reasons - especially this generation. I was so moved by the girl's desire to help me. I decided to share the story for everyone to know that, there are still good Samaritans out there. God is good.
Imagine how beautiful this world would be - if we all help each other and yes, even strangers!

And guess what her name was...GRACE.

She introduced herself as GRACE. Pure angel! Matthew 5:16 says,
"*In the same way, let your good deeds shine out for all to see, so that everyone will praise your heavenly Father*"

I know these days, helping strangers can actually get you in a lot of trouble. I have heard of stories where people sue or accuse good Samaritans of "wrongdoing", but please don't let that stop you.

If you help a stranger and if you do it "out of the goodness of your heart" and without any evil motives, God WILL protect YOU from ungrateful strangers. Reach out and help someone today. Your reward is in Heaven.

Demonic attacks

If you are a servant of God and you never get demonic attacks, you never experience trials and tribulations, if everyone loves you and life is always "a bed of roses" for you, you must reevaluate your Spiritual life. Because something is seriously wrong somewhere.

Understand that Satan never attacks his own children. So, for Satan to consider you one of his own - you must be doing something wrong as a Christian! Reevaluate your life.

When you GENUINELY open your heart to God, when you GENUINELY GIVE yourself to God, Satan begins to SHAKE in his boots because he foresees where God is TAKING you. He KNOWS he is in trouble and that is when Satan begins his numerous attacks on you. Think about it: What didn't Satan "throw" at Job??? Satan attacked everything in Job's life; Satan attacked his marriage, his business, his children, his property, the list goes on.

Through it all, Job didn't entertain anger and BITTERNESS in his heart, Oh no, instead, he HELD ON TO GOD, because he knew his reward would surely come from God. He knew Satan wouldn't have cared about attacking him if he wasn't GENUINELY SERVING God. He knew God would FIGHT for him!

Philippians 1:29 says;

"*For you have been given not only the privilege of trusting in Christ but also the privilege of suffering for him*"

Remember to FORGIVE the people Satan uses in attacking you.

Choose your words carefully

I'm a strong believer of "calling it like it is", "calling a spade a spade" and "confronting issues head on". I have always believed that if "little red flags" are ignored, it grows overtime inside a person's heart and transforms into a huge grudge or worse. Soon or later, that "little red flag" becomes a gigantic problematic balloon and bursts into a much greater flag. I have always "spilled my guts", I always spoke up and said whatever I was thinking and feeling.

Of course, there were times when I realized - right after I had "spilled my guts" - that maybe, I could've applied a little break to my lips or I could've been just a little bit patient.

But God has brought me far. Now, I actually calm down first, pray about it and THINK about what I need to say BEFORE I say it!

God has thought me to CHOOSE my words CAREFULLY!

Jesus said in Matthew 15:9-11 that,

"It's not what goes into your mouth that defiles you; YOU ARE DEFILED BY THE WORDS THAT COME OUT OF YOUR MOUTH."

Jesus went on to say in Matthew 15:17-20 that,

"Anything you eat passes through the stomach and then goes into the sewer. But the words you speak come from the heart—that's what defiles you. For from the heart come evil thoughts, murder, adultery, all sexual immorality, theft, lying, and slander. These are what defile you. Eating with unwashed hands will never defile you."

I am not asking you to harbor issues inside your heart and pretend all is well. No. You should always discuss and address matters - in order to avoid the problem from growing on you and becoming PROBLEMS. Keeping stuff inside will only cause you to explode one day - over something really small and that will ruin your friendships and relationships. It might even cause you to sin. And if you don't speak up, people will not know what's bothering you. They can't read your mind. You should always speak up - to the RIGHT PERSON though. Not behind their back...because, then it becomes gossip.

I am asking you to THINK about it, PRAY over the issue and ASK God's help in CHOOSING YOUR WORDS CAREFULLY - BEFORE you address the issue. That way, you won't sin against God and man. It is my prayer that God will take absolute and total control of your thoughts and your tongues.

Share Your Faith

The Christian confidence and faith is gradually dissolving and disappearing from our society. Christians shy away from sharing their faith in all circumstances. Gone are the days when you hear people wishing others “Merry Christmas”, instead, they say “Happy holidays”. We know Jesus Christ IS the REASON for that particular season – so how can we be afraid to freely say the words “Merry Christmas”? Majority of Christians are not confident enough to display and share their faith with others. They easily compromise with society by hiding their true faith. They are afraid to share the word with their friends, family and perhaps even strangers. Our Lord and Savior Jesus Christ have given every Christian His blessing and power to go preach the gospel.

We are to win the souls of unbelievers and to help them experience the saving power of the powerful blood of Jesus Christ. We are to help unbelievers establish a personal relationship with Jesus Christ. The least we can do is to stir them to the right direction – God’s direction. Most of us believers got saved because another Christian boldly followed the instructions of Jesus Christ in and preached and in some cases - lived the word with us. We are servants of God and we must do as God has directed and help save those who are lost.

You can also save a soul by your actions. Yes your actions must constantly speak volumes – your actions must scream every word of God to the unbeliever.

For example; don't gossip about others, don't cheat or try to deceive others and for Christ's sake don't tell lies. A lie always catches up with you. One lie always leads to another lie and another lie and another lie, before you know it, the lie has gotten way out of hand. You will find yourself constantly working hard to cover up a lie with another lie. Bad!

One thing I am gradually learning about when dealing with people, is that no one is perfect, it doesn't matter how old they are or what their title is – they are just as imperfect as you and me, so don't bad-mouth anyone. Because you are a Christian, your credibility will be permanently destroyed - if you preach one thing and do another. Most Christians lose confidence in sharing the gospel with others for different reason.

The scriptures wrote:

"Jesus came and told his disciples, "I have been given all authority in heaven and on earth. Therefore, go and make disciples of all the nations, baptizing them in the name of the Father and the Son and the Holy Spirit. Teach these new disciples to obey all the commands I have given you. And be sure of this: I am with you always, even to the end of the age." - Matthew 28:18-20

CHAPTER 9

GRACE

In Exodus 20:19, the Israelites said to Moses,

"You speak to us, and we will listen. But don't let God speak directly to us, or we will die!"
God warned Moses in Exodus 19:21-22 to "Go back down and warn the people not to break through the boundaries to see the Lord, or they will die. Even the priests who regularly come near to the Lord must purify themselves so that the Lord does not break out and destroy them."
You see, back then, God SPOKE to the Israelites THROUGH Moses.

They weren't allowed to approach the presence of God by themselves. They HAD to go through Moses to get to God. Our God is MERCIFUL. Bible says,

"*God showed His great love for us by sending Christ to die for us while we were still sinners. And since we have been made right in God's sight by the blood of Christ, He will certainly save us from God's condemnation*".... Romans 5:8-9.

Now that we have been saved by His amazing grace through the blood of Jesus Christ, God has granted us the right, honor, and privilege to be called His heir and to approach His throne - BY OURSELVES - CONFIDENTLY - ANYTIME, and ask HIM whatever we want. God even speaks to some of us! We are truly blessed. Let's not take that privilege for granted. Take full advantage of this great honor and PRAY CONTINUALLY. Think over your life. Ponder over the happiness, sadness, good, bad, disappointments, and everything that occurred throughout your life and you will realize that God has been with you through it all and on top of that, God gave you GRACE - time and time again. Take advantage by having a true RELATIONSHIP with God.
Have numerous conversations with your father - God - anytime!
Pray with confidence - making sure you are also living every word of wisdom from God's WORD.

Angels on earth

When I was pregnant with my first child, I went into labor around 2am and my husband called my doctor who asked us to meet her at the Hospital. When we got to the hospital, I believe there were two nurses at the nurse's station and they asked us to wait for a while, according to them, the hospital was full and there were no rooms available. I was in labor and driving to a different hospital wasn't an option.

Besides, that was the hospital my doctor had suggested and she was on her way to meet with us there. While my husband was going back and forth with the nurses and pleading with them to find me a room, another nurse appeared from nowhere and walked straight to me and she introduced herself as "Susie" (For privacy reasons, I will not include her last name).

After the introduction, Susie asked what was going on and we told her about the room situation, she said "I am sorry to hear that, I will be back shortly". After about 2 minutes, Susie was able put me in a room, asked who my doctor was, communicated with my doctor, and got me situated comfortably. She stayed with me.

My doctor arrived shortly afterwards. I started calling her Auntie Susie and I still do. She never left my side. She worked hand in hand with my doctor throughout my entire stay at the hospital.

After my baby and I got discharged, Auntie Susie visited us at home regularly teaching me how to handle my first baby, bringing us food and gifts. Calling and checking on us regularly. Shortly after that we got to meet her beautiful family also and they all continued to show us love.
We didn't know this wonderful woman from "Adam". Yet she was more than an angel to us. She showed true love to total strangers - us.

Auntie Susie was and still is a living example of the LOVE the bible talks about in Proverbs 3:3-4; "*Never let loyalty and kindness leave you! Tie them around your neck as a reminder. Write them deep within your heart. Then you will find favor with both God and people, and you will earn a good reputation*".

God blessed us in so many ways through this wonderful woman.
Psalm 91:11-12 says, "*For He will order His angels to protect you wherever you go. They will hold you up with their hands so you won't even hurt your foot on a stone*"

For us, Auntie Susie was the angel God sent to us. I don't know what we would have done if God hadn't brought her into our lives at that particular time. It was a perfect timing.

But of course, everything God does is perfect timing. He is never late and He never makes mistakes.

I can tell you a lot of stories about many angels God has brought into our lives over the years.

But I want you to get in the habit of respecting and appreciating everyone God brings into your life. Because that person could be the angel God has sent to you.

Sometimes, God also sends angels whom we must help. Be careful not to miss the opportunity of helping one of God's angels, because by so doing, you will also miss the blessings of God on the way to you.

Hebrews 13:2 says,
"*Don't forget to show hospitality to strangers, for some who have done this have entertained angels without realizing it!*"

This page was intentionally left blank

PART 3

A WORLD OF INSPIRATIONS

"A Collection of my Sermons"

CHAPTER 10

Betrayal

Satan was known as Lucifer prior to him wanting to be equal with God. When Satan tried to overthrow God and take over in heaven, Bible says one-third of the angels in heaven stood with Satan and rebelled against God. (Revelation 12:4). They failed miserably of course.

Revelations 12:8 says,

"And the dragon lost the battle, and he and his angels were forced out of heaven"
In Luke 10:18 Jesus said, *"I saw Satan fall from heaven like lightning!"*
Judas also betrayed Jesus in Luke 22:47-48.

Bible says in Numbers 16:1-3, that *"Korah son of Izhar, a descendant of Kohath son of Levi, conspired with Dathan and Abiram, the sons of Eliab, and On son of Peleth, from the tribe of Reuben, incited a rebellion against Moses, along with 250 other leaders of the community, all prominent members of the assembly. They united AGAINST Moses and Aaron".*

King David's son Absalom rebelled against his own father too. Disloyalty, backstabbing and betrayal didn't start with you and me. It started a zillion years ago in heaven. So if you have been betrayed, disappointed or if your most trusted confidant has rebelled against you, don't beat yourself up for trusting that person.

Don't even regret opening your heart for them. God lead them into your life for a reason. Don't worry. Remember that God himself has experienced a rebellion. Forgive them without holding any grudges and close that chapter of your life. The Lord God of Heaven's Armies will fight that battle for you.

The Red Sea

There was a time in my life when I hit what I call "my red sea". I felt as though I had been locked inside a little box and there was no way out.
I found myself in this predicament, this hole, and I didn't have the power to change a thing. Nothing and no human could help me even if they were willing to do so. In fact, I only saw a "lose – lose" situation for me - no matter what I did.
The only option I had was to look up and call on my God in heaven. So I worshiped, I cried, I fasted, I remembered my father's promise in Psalm 50:15, *"Call on me when you are in trouble, and I will rescue you, and you will give me glory."*

But then I heard the voice of Satan trying to convince me. Satan said to me "you know you are in denial?" "God is not coming to help you" "how long have you been praying and calling him?" "Where is He?""Give up"
I almost listened to Satan's lies.
You see, I actually agreed with Satan by thinking…. "Giving up isn't a bad idea".
But then MY GOD ALSO SPOKE to me. I closed my bedroom door, got on my bed face up and got on my laptop and started playing worship songs on YouTube.
While I was listening to the worship songs, my Omnipotent, Omnipresent, Jehovah El Shaddai reminded me of a covenant He made with me some time back in Isaiah 41:1-4 and 8-14.

He said; *"Listen in silence before me, you lands beyond the sea. Bring your strongest arguments. Come now and speak. The court is ready for your case. "Who has stirred up this king from the east, rightly calling him to God's service? Who gives this man victory over many nations and permits him to trample their kings underfoot?*
With his sword, he reduces armies to dust.
With his bow, he scatters them like chaff before the wind. He chases them away and goes on safely, though he is walking over unfamiliar ground. Who has done such mighty deeds, summoning each new generation from the beginning of time?
It is I, the Lord, the First and the Last. I alone am he." "But as for you, Israel my servant, Jacob my chosen one, descended from Abraham my friend, I have called you back from the ends of the earth, saying, 'You are my servant.' For I have chosen you and will not throw you away. Don't be afraid, for I am with you. Don't be discouraged, for I am your God. I will strengthen you and help you. I will hold you up with my victorious right hand. "See, all your angry enemies lie there, confused and humiliated. Anyone who opposes you will die and come to nothing. You will look in vain for those who tried to conquer you. Those who attack you will come to nothing. For I hold you by your right hand— I, the Lord your God. And I say to you, 'Don't be afraid. I am here to help you. Though you are a lowly worm, O Jacob, don't be afraid, people of Israel, for I will help you.
I am the Lord, your Redeemer. I am the Holy One of Israel.'

I knew right then that, yes, my God has spoken and made a covenant with ME and when God speaks its FINAL, NO ONE CAN CHANGE IT.

Anytime we are down, depressed and desperate, Satan sees an opportunity to strike. That is when Satan preys on our vulnerability. Arm yourself with the word of God and lots of prayers – especially when you find yourself depressed or when you find yourself struggling to hold onto your faith. Don't fall victim to Satan's games.

Prayer

Sometimes prayer becomes a very difficult thing to do when we are going through hard times. We decide not to pray because we either don't feel like praying or we simply cannot find the words or the energy to pray. But, it is essential that we pray - especially when we don't feel like it.
It is imperative that we pray when times are tough.
But if the words refuse to come, pray the Lord's prayer in Matthew 6:9-13;
"*Our Father in heaven, Hallowed be Your name. Your kingdom come. Your will be done. On earth as it is in heaven. Give us this day our daily bread. And forgive us our debts, As we forgive our debtors. And do not lead us into temptation, but deliver us from the evil one. For yours is the kingdom and the power and the glory forever Amen*"

If you can't remember the words for the prayer above, sing a few worship and praise songs. Most gospel songs are actually very powerful prayer songs. Understand that Satan knows that if you pray, God will show up and that's why he will do everything in his power to keep you from praying. It is up to YOU to push yourself to pray always. Pray even when all is well.
1 Thessalonians 5:16-18 tells us to;
"*Always be joyful. Never stop praying. Be thankful in all circumstances, for this is God's will for you who belong to Christ Jesus*".
Prayer is the only weapon to win any
Battle - Spiritual or physical.

Put God First

W e all love being "in control" of everything. We like to be in control of our lives, our jobs, and our families. Some of us can't just relax and allow someone else to "pamper us" for even a day...and that's either because we are not used to others caring for us or because we just love being "in control". There's nothing wrong with any of that. But life has many phases; happiness, love, joy, strong, brokenness, challenging and sad times. Life sometimes hits us with its very hardest phase, so hard that we just don't have the power to handle it. So we inevitably lose control.
I know you know what I'm talking about, because, it doesn't matter whether you are rich or poor, black or white, none of us are immune to it.

If you haven't yet experienced the hardest phase, you will. The Prophet Jeremiah prayed in Jeremiah 10:23-24;

"*I KNOW, LORD, THAT OUR LIVES ARE NOT OUR OWN. WE ARE NOT ABLE TO PLAN OUR OWN COURSE. So correct me, Lord, but please be gentle. Do not correct me in anger, for I would die*"

We must all be in agreement with Prophet Jeremiah and acknowledge the fact that our lives are truly not our own.

We must understand that no matter how hard we plan, if God disagrees with our plan, it just won't happen.

Always consult with God about your plans. Lose control and allow God to take total control of EVERYTHING in your life. He will change our plans whether we like it or not.

So why not step back and allow Him to step in?

Always put God first and everything else will follow.

It's A New Day

It doesn't matter what we did or didn't do yesterday, we are still alive because God has redeemed us today, and He has swept our sins away like the morning mist and given us another chance to start over by allowing us to see another beautiful day!.

Isaiah 44:22-23 says;

"I have swept away your sins like a cloud. I have scattered your offenses like the morning mist. Oh, return to me, for I have paid the price to set you free. Sing, O heavens, for the Lord has done this wondrous thing. Shout for joy, O depths of the earth!"

Today, I want to remind you that God has scheduled blessings for each and every one of His children. If your life is a constant mess because things aren't going right for you, yet your neighbor seems to be basking in constant blessings, my advice to you is to be truly happy for that neighbor. Don't be envious of them at all.

Don't be hateful. Rejoice with them. Keep in mind that, your own blessing is on the way and it will arrive just in God's scheduled time.

Even if you feel "forgotten", trust me, God can never forget you. If every hair on your heard is numbered, how can He forget your whole existence? (Mathew 10:30)

Isaiah 49:15 says,
"Never! Can a mother forget her nursing child? Can she feel no love for the child she has borne? But even if that were possible, I WOULD NOT FORGET YOU!"

Remember, God's TIMING IS ALWAYS THE BEST. Trust Him. Know that though all is not well with you,

God will see you through it all. Don't stop praising and thanking Him for what He has done for you. Make sure you "disappear" and allow God to take over completely. Keep in mind that it's all about Him. He is in control.

That way you can HEAR Him when He speaks, recognize His hands when you see them and feel His presence when He shows up!

Setting Priorities

"*I said to myself, "I will watch what I do and not sin in what I say. I will hold my tongue when the ungodly are around me. But as I stood there in silence— not even speaking of good things— the turmoil within me grew worse. The more I thought about it, the hotter I got, igniting a fire of words: Lord, remind me how brief my time on earth will be. Remind me that my days are numbered—how fleeting my life is*"...Psalm 39:1-4

Have you ever felt that way before? Have you ever made a decision to hold your tongue in a situation, but you still find yourself burning with words of anger within?......What do you do? Do you give in?

Well, King David seems to have been in a great distress at the time of this prayer in Psalm 39:1-4, but he composed himself with great restraint. He didn't allow himself to "loose it" and "go off". He had his priorities set - God FIRST. His salvation with God was more important than whatever had him "boiling" inside, and he allowed God's WORD to take precedence over the situation at hand.

As Matthew 6:33-34 says,
"*Seek the Kingdom of God ABOVE ALL ELSE, and LIVE RIGHTEOUSLY, and he will give you everything you need*"

Romans 12:2 states; *"Don't copy the behavior and customs of this world, but let God transform you into a NEW PERSON by CHANGING THE WAY YOU THINK. Then you will learn to know God's will for you, which is good and pleasing and perfect*".

Let us all LEARN from King David. When we are in distress or when we get upset, we must also exercise restraint and patience, allowing God's word to flow in our hearts.

In the Prophet Habakkuk's prayer, he said; "*EVEN THOUGH the fig trees have no blossoms, and there are no grapes on the vines; EVEN THOUGH the olive crop fails, and the fields lie empty and barren; EVEN THOUGH the flocks die in the fields, and the cattle barns are empty, YET I WILL REJOICE IN THE LORD! I WILL BE JOYFUL IN THE GOD OF MY SALVATION! THE SOVEREIGN LORD IS MY STRENGTH! He makes ME as surefooted as a deer, ABLE TO TREAD UPON THE HEIGHTS*"....Habakkuk 3:17-19.

Always put God first. Make every day a day of WORSHIP. Know that no matter what comes our way, we must trust God enough to BOLDLY DECLARE and CLAIM Habakkuk's prayer as our own.

We must PRAY...like this; EVEN THOUGH we are facing big challenges, EVEN THOUGH the mountains we face may be huge, EVEN THOUGH we may be facing constant trials and hardship, EVEN THOUGH we may be struggling with faith due to serious challenges in our lives and EVEN THOUGH our situation seems hopeless, YET I WILL REJOICE IN THE LORD! I WILL BE JOYFUL IN THE GOD OF MY SALVATION! THE SOVEREIGN LORD IS MY STRENGTH! He makes ME as surefooted as a deer, ABLE TO TREAD UPON THE HEIGHTS! EVEN THOUGH. TRUST IN THE LORD MY FRIENDS! I always say, as FAR as MY God has BROUGHT me, I'd be a fool to give up now. Think about just how FAR God has brought YOU and know that giving up now would be silly. HANG onto His every word. HANG ON to God, CONFIDENTLY KNOWING that EVEN THOUGH the earth crushes around you, you will stand tall and unscathed, REJOICING IN THE LORD!

This world has become a scary place. It's hard to know where to go because you never know what might happen there. We've got people killing each other, bombings here and there, earthquakes, hurricanes, tornadoes, children rebelling against parents, men sleeping with men, women sleeping with women, families rising against families, children being molested by "sick and deranged" adults, children killing children, and so on.

The amazing thing is that, Jesus prophesied about all these things 2000 years ago. Mark 13 shows how Jesus foretold His disciples the future, and it's all happening now. *"He said, "Nation will go to war against nation, and kingdom against kingdom. There will be earthquakes in many parts of the world, as well as famines. But this is only the first of the birth pains, with more to come"*

Jesus said in Mark 13:14; *"The day is coming when you will see the sacrilegious object that causes desecration standing where he should not be."*
Such as the "Satan statue" they put up in Detroit. They even have a "church of Satan" in the United States - Precisely Texas and New York. Everything is happening just as the Lord said it would. Take the time to read the whole book of Mark 13. Bible tells us that when all these things happen, WE must know that our Lord's RETURN is very NEAR. We must be READY. Are you ready? We must REPENT NOW - BEFORE He returns. NOW is the time. Don't wait until it's too late. Jesus is reminding you that He IS coming very SOON. Change your ways TODAY. Doesn't matter how badly you have messed up. Today is a new day.

Today, God is giving you ANOTHER CHANCE to change your ways. He has opened His hands to welcome you and ALL of your messes. He is offering you unfailing love, mercy, grace and Favor. I hope you will heed to His call.

Boldness and Humility in God

In Genesis 18, Abraham tried to reason with God about destroying the righteous along with the wicked with regards to Sodom and Gomorrah. Abraham started the bargaining at 50 and ended at 10. But he treaded each step carefully with humility and respect.

Genesis 18:20-33 states;

"So the Lord told Abraham, "*I have heard a great outcry from Sodom and Gomorrah, because their sin is so flagrant. I am going down to see if their actions are as wicked as I have heard. If not, I want to know. The other men turned and headed toward Sodom, but the Lord remained with Abraham. Abraham approached him and said, "Will you sweep away both the righteous and the wicked? Suppose you find fifty righteous people living there in the city—will you still sweep it away and not spare it for their sakes? Surely you wouldn't do such a thing, destroying the righteous along with the wicked. Why, you would be treating the righteous and the wicked exactly the same! Surely you wouldn't do that! Should not the Judge of all the earth do what is right?*"

And the Lord replied, "If I find fifty righteous people in Sodom, I will spare the entire city for their sake." (Keep reading through verse 33)

Abraham's boldness with total humility towards God - gives me the confidence that we can also approach the Lord with the most humility and respect to plead our own cases and just as Abraham intervened to save Lot, we can also intervene on behalf of others, because sometimes, God's mercy can trump his own judgment for His children. God listened to Abraham. He will listen to us too. He loves all of His children equally!

Do not give up. Plead your case with God.

Raise your kids in the Lord

We cannot choose the biological families we are born into. We have no control over that. Only God decides who will be our parents and siblings. Our parents also didn't have a choice in the children they bring into this world and they did their best to raise us, the best way they know how. And many of them made lots of mistakes with us that they may not even have realized.

While we cannot choose our family, we can choose our spouses and build our nuclear families.
Of course the ideal thing to do is ask God for wisdom and direction in choosing a life partner.

But unfortunately, we sometimes proceed without the Lord's input in the matter - hence making grave life mistakes. Just like our parents, we also do not get to choose our kids and our kids don't get to choose their siblings. God decides that. But we can choose to learn from our parents' mistakes and try to do better with our own kids. As good parents, we should only want our kids to do BETTER, be SMARTER and more SUCCESSFUL than we are.

We must raise our children in the way of the Lord. We must teach them the truth about God's Word. We must walk the talk, because they are WATCHING us daily.

Deuteronomy 6:6-9 says;

"And you must commit yourselves wholeheartedly to these commands that I am giving you today. Repeat them again and again to your children. Talk about them when you are at home and when you are on the road, when you are going to bed and when you are getting up. Tie them to your hands and wear them on your forehead as reminders. Write them on the doorposts of your house and on your gates".

Our children learn more by watching us. So let's be mindful of the way we interact with our spouses: the words we use at home such as CURSING and INSULTING each other. We can teach our children all we want. But in the end, they WILL DO what they see us doing on a daily basis.

Also, even if we didn't experience togetherness and love with our siblings, let's make it a priority to teach our kids to love one another.

The KEY to God's favor

You must cruise through life, knowing that God is STILL YOUR shepherd and YOUR STRENGTH. I want to encourage you to think, believe, and see life as David and Habakkuk did in the bible - they both trusted God COMPLETELY.
David said in Psalm 18:33;
"He makes me as surefooted as a deer, enabling me to stand on mountain heights"

Habakkuk also said in Habakkuk 3:19;
"*The Sovereign Lord is my strength! He makes me as surefooted as a deer, able to tread upon the heights*".

Now, that's what I call confidence in the Lord! When you adopt this kind of confidence in God, you KNOW it's all about Him. You KNOW He's on your side and NOTHING can hinder your blessings. You surrender COMPLETELY to Him - KNOWING you can also "STAND ON MOUNTAIN HEIGHTS". Commit EVERYTHING you do to the Lord. Go before Him with EVERY decision you want to make PRIOR to acting on that decision. Oh, and please PRAY OFTEN.

Prayer has always been the KEY to God's favor. Do this all from the core of your soul and not because I said so. God loves us so much that He never allowed any of the devil's weapons against us to succeed. God has kept you alive and well throughout another year.

But, are you READY for His coming? If He shows up this instance, will He find you righteous? Will He find you acceptable and holy?
Will He call you "my good and faithful servant"? (Matthew 25:23) Or will He deny knowing you?

(Matthew 7:23; "*But I will reply, 'I never knew you. Get away from me, you who break God's laws*")

Well, I pray you are ready. Because ready or not - He IS coming. No one can hide or run from Him.

1 Thessalonians 5:2 states;
"*For you know quite well that the day of the Lord's return will come unexpectedly, like a thief in the night*"

When He comes;
* for those who are NOT ready; Mathew 25:46 says, "And they will go away into eternal punishment" - (Hell)
* for those who ARE ready; the very same Mathew 25:46 says,
"But the righteous will go into eternal life" - (Heaven)

Now is the time to change. Now is the time to repent.

God has set you apart

Many companies are either doing a merger, downsizing or closing down a lot - lately and as a result, thousands of people have been laid off, terminated or forced to take pay-cuts. People are losing their jobs and that can be frustrating. I know of at least four companies who are currently laying employees off. About 90% of the people losing their jobs have families to take care of and bills to pay.
If you have been affected by this predicament, don't worry.
You are probably thinking: "how can I not worry when I have to feed my family and the bills need to get paid?"
Well, God gave me this message to be delivered "specially" for you;
He said for you to "*Look at the birds. They don't plant or harvest or store food in barns, for your heavenly Father feeds them. And aren't you far more valuable to him than they are?*"...Mathew 25:26.
God wants to know: "*Can all your worries add a single moment to your life*?"....Mathew 25:27

Then in Mathew 25:28 He asks again;
"*And why worry about your clothing? Look at the lilies of the field and how they grow. They don't work or make their clothing, yet Solomon in all his glory was not dressed as beautifully as they are?*"

God refers you back to verse 25, He said, "*THAT IS WHY I TELL YOU NOT TO WORRY about everyday life—whether you have enough food and drink, or enough clothes to wear*".

Lastly, God is reminding you of a very important fact that you may have forgotten and that fact can be found in Jeremiah 1:5, He said;

"*I KNEW YOU BEFORE I FORMED YOU in your mother's womb. BEFORE YOU WERE BORN I SET YOU APART and appointed you as my prophet to the nations.*"

Besides, who gave you the job you just lost in the first place? If you think you got that job just because of your qualifications, think again!
There were people better qualified for that job who also interviewed for the same job, but God gave the job to YOU.
All He is asking is for you to TRUST HIM AGAIN. Can you do that?

Food for thought

We have the tendency of taking delight in hearing or seeing the downfall of others. Amazingly, we actually take pleasure in the pain and suffering of others. Some of us are anxiously waiting for that faithful day - when we get to hear bad news about our "friends" or "family members".

If you love seeing another person's life destroyed, beware. While that person's misfortune may have arrived today, your own misfortune may be on its way to you. The few years I have spent in this world have taught me just how tiny and round this world can be.

If you are waiting for bad news about someone, be careful, what you wish for that friend or family member may end up being your own fate.

Keep in mind that only God knows our tomorrow. That person may have fallen today, but their tomorrow might be extremely brighter and greater than yours.

In fact, they might even be your future stepladder to the blessings God has planned for you.

Proverbs 17:5 says;

"Those who mock the poor insult their Maker; those who rejoice at the misfortune of others will be punished"

Proverbs 24:17-18 also states;

"Don't rejoice when your enemies fall; don't be happy when they stumble. For the Lord will be displeased with you and will turn his anger away from them"

Wish everyone well. Bless everyone God brings into your way. If someone falls, their life is over. That might even be God's blessings in disguise for them.

God will fight for you

Some of us are always praying, fasting and reading the Bible. We know every word in the Bible from genesis to revelation. And that's great. The problem is that, the minute we finish praying or fasting or reading the Bible, we get into an argument or fight with our spouses, friends, family, strangers or neighbors. We are always angry with someone for something.
Our hearts are full of hatred, grudges and plans of revenge.
And even though we know every word in the bible, we still push them all aside and take matters into our own hands and we find ourselves speaking foolishly.
I once heard someone say;
"*I am a Christian, but I have no problem putting my bible aside and beating you*".

Another person also said;
"I used to worship idols prior to converting to Christianity and I will gladly put down my bible and have those idols curse and kill you"........
REALLY?! ☺

I know it sounds like a "soap opera".
But sadly it's true. Some of us actually say and do things like that!
There is no way you can be a Christian and talk like that. Understand that love is a requirement for every Christian.

The God we serve IS LOVE and He commands us to give love accordingly.

John 15:12-13;
"*This is my commandment: Love each other in the same way I have loved you. There is no greater love than to lay down one's life for one's friends*".

Let's love one another.
Allow God to fight your battles for you.

Love God more

A couple was driving on a small road and they saw a 16 year old girl who was hitchhiking. A voice told the man (the man was driving) to pull over and pick the girl up. But when he told his wife what he was about to do, his wife objected to the idea. So he listened to his wife and didn't pick up the girl. Shortly after that, they almost died in a car accident, but they were saved by a man who introduced himself as Jesus - son of God. Jesus told them that although the man had served him faithfully all his life, his wife doesn't know Jesus and gave her a chance to repent.

He also said to the man;
"*You disobeyed me when I asked you to pick up that girl on the road because your wife disagreed. You must listen to my voice over anyone else's - including your wife's voice - your wife doesn't know me*".

It's good to listen to our spouses. But when your spouse happens to be an unbeliever, and their advice opposes God's instructions, we must not adhere to them. God's voice MUST trump theirs. Proverbs 5:1-6 says,
"My son, pay attention to my wisdom; listen carefully to my wise counsel. Then you will show discernment, and your lips will express what you've learned"
Love your spouse. But love God more. Instead of listening to your unbelieving spouse, pray for them to repent. You'd be amazed what God can do!

Have you figured it out yet?

We have been hearing about Jesus Christ, His earthly ministry, and the awesome miracles He performed here on earth and how he came to die for our sins. Most of us have even been blessed enough to actually EXPERIENCE miracles and breakthroughs from Him in our own lives. Some of us have also repented from our sins and accepted Him as our Lord and personal Savior.
Some of us are even spreading His WORD to the world.

Matthew 16:13-19 states,

" *When Jesus came to the region of Caesarea Philippi, he asked his disciples, "Who do people say that the Son of Man is?" "Well," they replied, "some say John the Baptist, some say Elijah, and others say Jeremiah or one of the other prophets."* " *Then he asked them, "BUT WHO DO YOU SAY I AM?"Simon Peter answered, "You ARE THE MESSIAH, THE SON OF THE LIVING GOD."* "*Jesus replied, "You are blessed, Simon son of John, because my Father in heaven has revealed this to you. You did not learn this from any human being*"

What about you my friend? You know of Him. But do you know Him?
DO YOU KNOW WHO HE IS YET?
Have you figured it out you? I pray your answer is a solid yes.

But if your answer is "no" or if your answer is a wavering "yes", I strongly suggest you begin with a prayer of genuine repentance - asking God for spiritual wisdom and insight, ask God for a deeper understanding of Him and His word.
Now your next step is to study the word of God in the Bible on a daily basis and pray often to SEEK His face.
Bible says IF you seek Him wholeheartedly, you will find Him.

Blessed to be alive

We are honored to be among the living. Our God is good. "*You are worthy, O Lord our God, to receive glory and honor and power. For you created all things, and they exist because you created what you pleased.*" - Revelation 4:11

Please pray with me,

Thank you Heavenly Father, for my life and the lives of every member of my family. Thank you for your favor, grace, mercies and Unfailing Love you bestow upon me daily. This week, please help me to live your every word as I interact with the people you bring my way, so that everyone will see your light shining through me.
Help me to win many souls to you, not just by what I say, but by what I do.

Daddy, please forgive my sins. Break me, fold me, shape me, cleanse me, mold me and use me for your glory. Strengthen my faith in you, so that no matter how dark things may seem, I will KNOW that you are STILL with me.
I thank you Lord. I love you Lord. Receive all the glory. Thank you for giving me the privilege to come before your throne of grace.

In Jesus' NAME I pray.

Amen.

CHAPTER 11

Checking Facts

When old friends met at a gathering, they began reminiscing about the past, which scooped up a topic on another friend named Benny, who wasn't present at that gathering. Nothing bad was said about Benny. A bystander named Lila overhead "Benny's" name in the conversation and though she didn't really hear the details of the conversation, she went and informed Benny that he was being discussed at the party and added a few juicy details that she didn't hear.

She also named every attendee who was present at the gathering.

Benny got very angry and instantly decided not to speak with any of his friends again. He didn't bother to check the facts before reacting to the HEARSAY. Lila also shouldn't have told Benny what she did not hear in the first place. The problem with gossip is that the message couriers usually don't have the facts of the message they are distributing. So their message is always hearsay.

Webster defines hearsay as: "something heard from another person: rumor".
Are you living your life based on "HEARSAY"?
Be very careful, "*he says - she says*" is dangerous.
Hearsay can lead one into a shameful disaster.

Most of the time, you'll find that, the facts are totally different from what you were originally told. Keep in mind that "rumors" loses its "truth" as it travels.
Check out the following Scriptures:
Exodus 23:1, *"You must not pass along false rumors. You must not cooperate with evil people by lying on the witness stand"*

Proverbs 18:8, *"Rumors are dainty morsels that sink deep into one's heart".*
Proverbs 16:28-29, *"A troublemaker plants seeds of strife; gossip SEPARATES the best of friends, violent people MISLEAD their companions, leading them down a harmful path".*

Remember "the golden rule" in Mathew 7:12, *"Do to others whatever you would like them to do to you".*
Before you react to hearsay, ask yourself this; "If the tables were turned, will I expect the person to check the FACTS before reacting against me?"
Another great thing is to ask the "info bearer" what role they played in the "story" they are bringing to you. Most of the time, after patiently investigating the matter, you will discover the "info bearers" are the true "gossipers".

My advice to you is to always check the FACTS before you act. Keep in mind that every story has two or more sides.

There are some pastors whose sermons are based on "private counseling" with members of their church. That's right; they bring private matters, disclosed to them in confidence and confidentially, to the pulpit on Sundays.

Some pastors also use their pulpit as a "boxing ring" to send "indirect messages" to the people they would like to "tell-off".

Others uses their pulpit to send replies to people for "something" - a gossiper had told them - that "someone said" about them.

(Pastors and church leaders shouldn't be entertaining and encouraging gossip anyway)

Please don't misunderstand me; There ARE some men/women of God whose sermons are SOLELY BASED ON THE WORD OF GOD - and sometimes the messages God gives them goes against some of us...but that's okay, because that message is God's word.

But for everyone else preaching whatever they want, beware, for there are consequences. Know that, by not preaching the word, YOU are hindering the Holy Spirit's work in the church, because the Holy Spirit works through the WORD of God.
Ephesians 6:17 clearly states, "*Put on salvation as your helmet, and take the SWORD OF THE SPIRIT, WHICH IS THE WORD OF GOD*"

2 Timothy 4:2 says, *"PREACH THE WORD of God. Be prepared, whether the time is favorable or not. Patiently correct, rebuke, and ENCOURAGE your* people with GOOD TEACHING"

This message is also for ANYONE preaching the "word" - whether you are a pastor or not, Make sure you are preaching the WORD God asks you to share and nothing else.

Prayer for sale

These days, if you ask some pastors to pray for you, they demand payment before they will pray for you. And they have "prayer packages" for sale. Some churches have silver, gold, platinum or diamond in prayer packages. So the type of prayer you get depends on how much money you pay them.

The amount you pay will determine the "quality" of the prayer you will get. I know it sounds fictional, but it's true.

My friends, you ought to know that if you must pay money to be prayed for, I can guarantee you that those "prayers" will NOT reach God's ears.

The Apostle Paul said;
*"Yet preaching the Good News is not something I can boast about. I am compelled by God to do it. How terrible for me if I didn't preach the Good News! If I were doing this on my own initiative, I would deserve payment. But I have no choice, for God has given me this sacred trust. What then is my pay? It is the opportunity to preach the Good News without charging anyone. That's why I never demand my rights when I preach the Good News"....*1 Corinthians 9:15-18

Jeremiah 8:11 says,

"They offer superficial treatments for my people's mortal wound. They give assurances of peace when there is no peace"

To those Pastors and Prophets, who are trying to manipulate the Holy Spirit; Matthew 10:8-9 says, "*Heal the sick, raise the dead, cure those with leprosy, and cast out demons. GIVE AS FREELY AS YOU HAVE RECEIVED! "DON'T TAKE ANY MONEY in your money belts—no gold, silver, or even copper coins*"

My dear friends, if there's a price tag on "prayer" for you, its commerce, trade and strictly business. God is not at that place. Do not pay for prayers. God gives **freely**.

YOU can also get on your knees, open your heart and talk to God - one on one. Yes, my friends, Yahweh WILL also hear you too! God has no favorites.

You don't have to be a pastor/prophet in order for God to answer YOUR prayers. Please don't encourage those fake people by paying for prayers.

Study the WORD - Yourself

The word of God is free and with the help of technology, it's all over the internet for grasps. Everybody translates God's word differently. Everyone preaches it differently. So you do not have to depend solely on someone to educate you on the dos and don'ts of God's word. Knowledge is everything.
Jesus said in Hosea 4:6, "*My people are destroyed for lack of knowledge. Because you have rejected knowledge, I also will reject you from being priest for me; because you have forgotten the law of your God, I also will forget your children.*"

When in doubt, study the word yourself. Ask God for spiritual insight and wisdom to help you understand His word. You'll be amazed how transformed you will become and how much you can learn in God's word. If there are any discrepancies in what you were taught by someone else, God will open your mind and your heart to see it and lead you to the right source of information. Unfortunately, too many people are misleading the children of God. They are tweaking and customizing the word of God to meet their own evil desire. They have all the facts well twisted.

Isaiah 9:15-16 describes such people this way, *"The elder and honorable, he is the head; the prophet who teaches lies, he is the tail. For the leaders of this people cause them to err, and those who are led by them are destroyed."*

If you feel uneasy about something you are being taught in the word of God, don't accept it. Get online, get a Bible and check all the facts on your own. Do your own research.

Ask God for discernment for His word. Ask God to show you how to serve Him better and genuinely. Ask Him to make you stronger in Him so that you don't end up falling for lies. Make prayer a part and parcel of your everyday life.

Earlier this week I watched a movie and in the movie there was a very powerful and successful pastor who performed many miracles in his church. One of his church members brought him a very wealthy man who had been declared hopeless by the Doctors and had been given couple of weeks to live. The pastor healed him and he didn't die. After the man was healed, he was so moved by the fact that God had healed him, that he repented and started praying and studying the word more often than before.

One day, God revealed to the wealthy man that, the pastor's miracles are not of God. God showed him that the pastor's church was built on evil rituals from a fetish priest and that He (God) had nothing to do with that Pastor's church. God started using the rich man for His glory.
So I wondered; why did God accept prayers from this rich man who went to a fake "man of God" for healing? Why has God made this rich man one of his prophets?

Though the story was a movie, because it is something that does occur in real life, the Holy Spirit answered my question: “Because the rich man DIDN'T KNOW that the pastor wasn't of God”. God healed the rich man because he truly believed that the Pastor was praying in the name of God and he believed that God would heal him. That’s why God healed him.

“God ALLOWED the healing to stick because of the man's faith that the pastor was a true representative of God”. But as soon as God revealed the truth to him, he quit that church because he now knew better.

I wanted to share this with you all and to inform you that; IF you KNOW that your Pastor is NOT of God, to the point that you even talk about him behind his back, yet you CONTINUE to worship with that Pastor, for whatever reason, YOU ARE SINNING AGAINST GOD and wasting your time. If you just want to fellowship, find an actual social club, because church is more than just for "fellowship".

Here's what the Bible says to YOU;
"*Dear friends, if we DELIBERATELY continue sinning after we have received KNOWLEDGE of the truth, there is no longer any sacrifice that will cover these sins*" - Hebrews 10:26.

Remember to check the facts in the Bible or online when in doubt.

This page was intentionally left blank

Chapter 12

Communication

I had two visits from an old acquaintance that I hadn't seen in a very long time. During her first visit, she started to tell me something very disturbing that she claimed another old acquaintance had said about me - regarding my visit to that person – some months prior. I had paid that other acquaintance a visit because God had moved an awesome mountain for him and when he told me about it, I went to celebrate with him and his family, because I was genuinely happy for what God had done for them.

But I told her I didn't really want to know whatever that person may or may not have said about me. She appeared embarrassed by my reaction and comments and took her leave peacefully. A few weeks later she paid me a visit again and she during her visit, she brought up the topic of the old acquaintance again.
This time even though I told her I didn't want to know, she blurted out exactly what she was obviously determined to tell me.
I ignored what I heard.

A few days later, I realized that her words had turned into seeds and had taken root in my heart. Her words were rapidly growing in my heart - because I found myself boiling the more I thought about what she claimed was said about me. Normally, I would address the issue right away because one thing I have always disliked is hearsay.
But as I contemplated about whether or not to address the issue, it hit me hard; I AM DOING THE EXACT SAME THING I PREACH AGAINST – HEARSAY! And I am granting Satan room inside my heart **based on something I heard!**

Then I remembered Isaiah 42:6,
"*"I, the LORD, have called you to demonstrate my righteousness."*
I also remembered Isaiah 11:3,
"He will delight in obeying the LORD. He will not judge by appearance nor make a decision based on hearsay"

Suddenly, I felt so ashamed of myself for even entertaining such childish nonsense. I said to myself; "I am a woman of God for Christ sake!"
I prayed and asked God to help me not to nurse any negative thoughts or feelings against the third party or the info bearer.
God answered me because He uprooted the growing seed and made a way for me to be able to communicate with the said party.

You see how badly I handled the whole thing? Yes. I allowed my "flesh and human side" to rule me, when I should have called on God FIRST. I should have allowed the insight and wisdom of God's word to operate in me – sooner rather than later. That is the mistake most of us make. It is easier for us to get angry, walk away and neglect proper and Christ like communication, than it is for us to communicate with the people who can set the record straight.

I remember many years ago, when a relative had moved in with us, about two weeks or so into her stay with us, I went to get my mail from our residential mailbox and I **habitually** opened all the mail prior to realizing that one of the mail I opened belonged to our new house guest. Upon that realization, I went to her and confessed that I had opened up her mail by accident, apologized and explained that I have a habit of opening up all the mail since the only mail we ever got was either for me or my husband.

I even told her it will not happen again since she now lives with us on a temporary basis.
After I was done speaking, she looked at me very sternly, got up, walked pass me and calmly climbed the stairs to her room.
She did not speak with me for two weeks. Instead, she called other people and talked about me.

I believe a simple communication with me about how she felt would have sufficed and would have been better than deforming my image to a third and fourth party.
I know siblings who aren't on speaking terms with each other due to lack of a simple communication. They either hate each other or are angry with each other...I'm not quite sure of what it is, but I am 110% sure that if they would just communicate with EACH OTHER about all the unnecessary "he say – she say drama", they will have the beautiful relationship God intended for families.

Many marriages and love relationships sadly crumbles due to lack of communication. Instead of communicating in our relationships, we tend to "think" for others. We think we already know what the person will say or do, when we might be totally wrong.
Communication, my friend, is crucial in any relationship. No relationship can survive without proper communication and honesty – no matter how hard the truth may sound.

There was a time in my marriage when I realized my husband and I appeared to be drifting apart.
I thought about our life together and the years we have shared together. Then I went to my husband and asked him to tell me the things I did in the beginning of our relationship which made him happy and the things I don't do anymore.
I promised to not get upset about his honest answer. He answered my questions.
He was honest and told me the things I had stopped doing over the years – things he loved about me. I also told him the things he had also stopped doing. I can tell you that, that type of **communication** made all the difference in our relationship.

Learn how to communicate with everyone in your life. Anybody who knows me really well will tell you that I have a really bad habit of not checking my voicemail regularly on my mobile phone. I only check my voicemail when I am expecting an urgent telephone call. Otherwise, I normally just wait till my voicemail becomes full and then I hit "delete all" to create more room.

I know you are asking; "why create more room if you don't check your voicemail?" Right?
I create more room because if I were to miss an urgent call, I would like to have the option of actually listening to that voicemail. ☺
Every close friend and family member knows to text me if I miss their call. Technology has me spoiled rotten.

Anyway, I hadn't heard from a family friend for about a week and I wasn't worried because I was under the impression that she was out of town.
I knew she'd contact me upon her return.
One morning I had a missed call from a potential employer I had emailed previously and I decided to check my voicemail before returning the call.

While listening to my messages, I stumbled into a voicemail from this family friend in question and the voicemail was about a week old.

Immediately, I contacted her and informed her that I just heard her voicemail. I explained to her that my phone never registered a missed call from her. I reminded her that I barely check my voice messages. Unknowingly to me, the reason she hadn't called me back since the day she left the voicemail was because, she had assumed that since she called me once and left me one voicemail and I never returned her call, "something was wrong with our friendship".
Apparently she had even decided to "walk away" - based on the assumption that I intentionally neglected to return her call.

Now, what if I hadn't checked my voicemail when I did? Or what if I had done a "delete all" to my messages like I usually do?

I never would have heard her voicemail and since I hadn't heard from her in a week, what if I had also assumed the worst and decided to "walk away"?

If we had both decided to walk away from each other based on the assumption that the other person is up to no good or had some sort of evil motive, the devil would have succeeded in destroying yet another relationship.

Assumptions can be dangerous.
No communication or **mis**communication can be even more dangerous. They can both be damaging to beautiful relationships. Assumption is defined as something that you assume to be the case, when in truth you have no proof whatsoever and you could be wrong.

If you don't understand something, please ASK questions. Don't assume.
Oh my friends, when you see a difference in your family or friend's actions, please do not **assume** they have something against **you** or that they are somehow upset with you – especially if you have done nothing wrong. For all you know, they might be going through something completely different– they might be battling something bigger than you, it might not be about you or your relationship. They might not even have realized that they have any changes in behavior.

When assumptions come, they bring company with them; they bring grudge, malice, anger, and hurt. If you are not careful, you will run off every good person God brings into your life – all based on ASSUMPTIONS.

Colossians 3:17,
"And whatever you do or say, do it as a representative of the Lord Jesus, giving thanks through him to God the Father"

God encourages His children to do everything in our power to live in PEACE with EVERYONE. Don't allow assumptions to drive you into war with the world.
We met this very beautiful couple who seemed powerful in the Lord. They seemed very sweet and our families became good friends. Everything was beautiful between the two families.
Then one day, suddenly, they began to change towards us.

For example, in the past, we would greet each other whenever we run into each other. But one day, we saw them standing in front of their garage, but immediately we tried to wave, they ignored us and quickly closed their garage.
There was another time we run into them on the streets while taking a walk and we tried to say hello, but they passed right by us as if we were strangers. They would see you standing on the left and they would change route to go right. We thought that was odd. I went to their home and I asked both of them if we had offended them in any way.
The woman responded in a very friendly manner. She said we had done nothing wrong.

Her husband didn't utter a word – which was odd too because he normally would have talked.

I told them they had changed toward my family and we are concerned because we had such a great relationship with them.
Again, the woman said they didn't realize they had changed and she reiterated the fact that we had not offended them in any way. Even though she said everything was fine, I got on my knees before her and I told her I was sorry if my family had offended them in any way. She told me to get up and insisted all was well. I got up and we hugged before I left.

She even told me that she was happy and appreciated the fact that I approached them with my concern and didn't sit on it.
She said I was a true friend and we hugged again. She even saw me to the door. I thought everything was truly fine. I was beginning to think that maybe we had misread their actions. But their odd actions didn't change at all after our communication. In fact, it got worst. We would call them and our calls would be automatically forwarded directly to voicemail. After a while, I eventually realized that they had blocked our calls on their phones. I went back to their house and sat with them again. I asked if everything was fine, again, the man kept quiet and the woman claimed all is well. She claimed we hadn't done anything wrong.

Again, I apologized to them for whatever we may have done – though she insisted that my husband and I hadn't offended them in any way.

We hugged again and I left. But they continued their new actions toward us. We prayed about it, left everything to God and decided to move on. But most importantly, we asked God to help us move on without any hurt, malice or grudge. And by God's grace, we have been able to move on and leave all that in the past.
One of the requirements of having the honor of being called a "child of God" is to be on good terms with everyone – IF it depends on YOU.
In fact, Hebrews 12:14 says,
" *Work at living in peace with everyone, and work at living a holy life*".
You are probably thinking; " *what if the person doesn't want to live in peace with me*?"...Or "Suppose I have tried everything in my power to resolve a dispute with someone - but nothing has worked, the person just won't listen"...

"What do I do now?"
Well, Conflict resolution is very crucial inside the family of Christ - in order for our blessings to flow and for our relationship with our father (God) to grow. If you KNOW in your heart, that you have truly done everything within your power to make peace with that individual and nothing has worked, my humble advice to you is to pray about the matter and leave it to our God - who always knows the end from the beginning.

He knew when you were created that, not everyone will always be on the same page with you. He only cares about your part in the matter.

He cares about how YOU - His child - will handle the matter. That's why He told us in Romans 12:18 that "*IF IT IS POSSIBLE, AS FAR AS IT DEPENDS ON YOU, live at peace with everyone*". God knows you cannot control another person's actions. However, before you pray about it, make sure you "*get rid of all bitterness, rage and anger, brawling and slander, along with every form of malice*".....Ephesians 4:31.

Move on with a CLEAN heart towards that person and continue praying for them. Make sure you have done EVERYTHING within your power to resolve any conflicts. But, like the couple I told you about, you cannot possibly resolve a conflict if the person insists "all is well", even though all is obviously not well.
You leave the matter to God because ONLY God can see our hearts and ONLY God knows best.

Side Attractions

Apostle Paul is one of my favorite Apostles because in all of his Christian life, he looked at things on earth from God's point of view. Because of this, he was never upset by the things behind him, around him, or before him. He never allowed "things or people" to rob him of his joy! He only cared about God's opinion. Never allow anyone or anything to rob you of your joy. Don't let the things behind you, around you or before you upset you and hinder your Blessings. Satan will use people to cause you to miss out on a great opportunity just by tormenting, provoking or upsetting you. Those people are side attractions Satan uses to derail you from the narrow road to God. I have learned never to dignify those side attractions with a response or reaction, because by responding to them, you are making them feel important, allowing them to distract you from your walk with God.

Learn to ignore the side attractions.

Hebrews 12:2 says;

" *We do this by keeping our eyes on Jesus, the champion who initiates and perfects our faith*"

Be prayerful and God will give you the grace to do without the "side attractions".

Caution: Satan is a very sour loser. So please expect him to keep trying. But don't let your guard down. Be Prayerful. Keep your eyes on God. Don't get distracted by Satan and his cohorts. Don't let anyone steal your joy. Be like Paul and start seeing things from God's point of view.

When God decides to bless you

A friend of mine wanted the opportunity to travel so badly. His hope was 100% banking on his rich uncle. For years he was sure of the fact that his dream would only happen through his uncle. And the uncle didn't disappoint him. He tried his best to make his nephew's dream come true. But for some reason, whatever his uncle tried failed.
His uncle's money didn't seem to make a difference this time. My friend got turned down numerous times for the visa he needed to travel to his dream country. He was heartbroken.
My friend finally gave up on his dreams.

Then one day, he met a total Stranger who took it upon herself to fulfill his dream. It just so happens that the stranger was from the country he so badly wanted to visit. So the stranger kept her word and my friend now lives in that country.
This was God all the way!
When God decides to bless you - he doesn't need any body's approval, he doesn't need to seek permission from anyone.
He doesn't need any body's help and absolutely NOTHING and NO ONE can stop His blessings for you.
He WILL bless you no matter what!

God said to Moses in Romans 9:15,
"*I will show mercy to anyone I choose, and I will show compassion to anyone I choose*".

I agree with the Prophet Isaiah when he said, "*Truly, O God of Israel, our Savior, you work in mysterious ways*".....Isaiah 45:15.

When God decides to favor you, my dear friend, you will be surprised at how He chooses to do it. Yes, He uses the unexpected to perform His mighty MIRACLES.
Depend Only on God.
Trust His Word.
God will AMAZE you with mighty miracles.

CHAPTER 13

Power & Leadership

My first management position was a complete disaster because my understanding of management and leadership was very different than what it ought to be.

My definition of leadership was to sit back, issue my commands and do things on the computer – which is absolutely nothing.

I thought because I was the boss, my job was to give orders and just supervise my team while they work. I also thought because I was the boss, none of my employees was allowed to stand up to me or voice out an opinion. I found out the hard way that I was wrong. I wasn't leading by example and that made me a bad boss. When you have a very unhappy team, no success can be attained. So my team was always on the losing side of goals. My office looked bad and that reflected badly on me.

Being powerful can be a good thing and it can also be a bad thing - depending on how it's used. Power can be used to save, achieve, protect and build. Power can also be used to kill, cheat, destroy, hurt, intimidate, manipulate, blackmail and abuse others. Some leaders will not hire or promote people unless they do despicable things for them.

There was a story in the news about a Catholic Priest who was caught with his pants down ready to have sex with a lady who had applied for a job from him. The "man of God" told the lady that the only way she would get the job was to sleep with him. Can you believe that nonsense?!
So the lady and her husband teamed up to set the Priest up. Good for them!

Most leaders abuse their power. Some of these leaders were humble until God elevated them and suddenly, they think they are bigger than God Himself. But our God is merciful and patience. So He watches them carefully and gives them numerous opportunities to repent. But they don't.

If God has made you powerful, whether through riches, title, status, or through a gift of the Holy Spirit - use it wisely.

Someday, God will hold you highly accountable. Be careful! 1 Peter 5:2 says;
"*Care for the flock that God has entrusted to you. Watch over it willingly, not grudgingly—not for what you will get out of it, but because you are eager to serve God*".

Don't misuse or abuse your power - for every one of us will definitely reap every single thing we sow here on earth.

Obadiah 15:16 says,
"*For the day of the Lord upon all the nations is near; as you have done, it shall be done to you; Your reprisal shall return upon your own head*".

A leader's confidence becomes arrogance when he forgets who made him a leader in the first and when he forgets the meaning of the word "humility". A great leader leads by example.

In Psalm 8, David teaches all leaders how to maintain both confidence and humility without being arrogant. He humbled himself and gave God His glory.
Yes, David fell numerous times, he messed up a thousand times, but the awesome thing is that, he always got right back up - with God holding his hand.

Like many of us, He was far from perfect.
In verses 3-4, King David acknowledged his own weakness and the fact that he's human.
He also points out our weaknesses as humans.

He said, "*When I consider Your heavens, the work of Your fingers, the moon and the stars, which You have ordained, what is man that You are mindful of him, And the son of man that You visit him*?"

King David respected and saw his position for what it was - God-given. He never forgot that God placed him on the throne.

Every leader, whether big or small, should never forget that without God, they would never have made it up there and without God, they will not stay there. God placed them there and God can bring them down any moment.

We should all understand that God can drop us any given second at His discretion. Let's replace any arrogance with confidence in the Lord. Ask God for the Spirit of humility and wisdom.

Like King David, let's magnify the Lord, giving Him all the credit for the great privilege of the honor of our lives and leadership.
Most importantly, people must see the light of God in us - always. Let's “walk the talk”.
Don’t preach red and live green.

Criticizing Leaders

We have all been there - done that. We have all criticized or judged leaders of a church. We all expect perfection from church leadership, due to some actions they have displayed or some things they have said. Granted, most Pastors, deacons, elders, and leaders of the church don't necessarily do what they ought to be doing. Most of them even do the opposite of what the Holy Bible clearly states. And some of them falter in ways that they shouldn't. All of the above could be due to them being "imperfect" or even "fake". But we are not in the position to make that judgment.

Only God can differentiate between the two. Whatever the case may be, it's not up to us to determine their fate, judge or criticize them. That's God's job.
In Numbers 12, Moses' siblings, Miriam and Aaron criticized Moses because he had married a Cushite woman. God heard them and He stepped in to defend His chosen one - Moses.
Numbers 12:6-10 says,
"*And the Lord said to them, "Now listen to what I say: If there were prophets among you, I, the Lord, would reveal myself in visions. I would speak to them in dreams. But not with my servant Moses. Of all my house, he is the one I trust. I speak to him face to face, clearly, and not in riddles! He sees the Lord as He is. So WHY WERE YOU NOT AFRAID TO CRITICIZE MY SERVANT Moses?"*

Bible says, The Lord was very angry with them, and he departed putting leprosy on Miriam's skin. If the "actions and attitudes" of your Church leadership begins to affect your spiritual growth negatively, pray to God for direction.
But do not go around gossiping, judging or backstabbing the Leader of that establishment.

Ask for God's direction and if God is NOT present in that church, He will remove you from that congregation peacefully and personally place you in a bible-based church - where God IS present. But if you decide not to exit the building, then please make a decision NOT to judge or criticize them.

How's Your Faith?

"Sometimes I feel too discouraged and too weak to go on, I feel like my faith is dropping rapidly, I feel like I just can't catch a break, oh I'm tired of holding on, I feel helpless, maybe I should just quit"…That was me whining to a friend after I had experienced disappointments after disappointments - within a very short time frame. I am not sure of what I expected to hear from my friend; Sympathy, empathy, comfort - maybe? But no, I didn't get any of that. What I did get from my friend was; "Naomi, I'm shocked to hear you speak like that, because I see you as this strong woman who's got everything under control, I hold you in very high esteem".
I must confess that his words, as weird as it may sound, encouraged me greatly. I realized just how low life was throwing me. I felt so down and weak emotionally and spiritually, yet I also felt ashamed for feeling that way.
I realized that I am not exempted from having my faith tested. Just like many great people in the Bible, none of us are exempted from having our faith tested.

Let's talk about David, it didn't matter that God chose him to be King Saul's successor and to rule over God's people; King Saul was seeking to kill David out of sheer jealousy, so David had to constantly run for his life. He had to keep hiding in caves.

Psalm 142 and many other Psalms tells us that David broke down and cried to God constantly, but David also praised God constantly at the end of the Psalms. David's faith got tested, David broke down, but he didn't stay down, he always got up by praising God at the end of each break down. He never gave up. He made God's word sovereign in his life each time his faith got tested.
How many times do we end up doing the very same thing we planned not to do?
I don't know about you, but I find myself doing exactly what I promised myself and God that I wouldn't do. I believe we all do. None of us "can do" anything by our own power – we need the Sovereign power of God to lead and empower us.

Take Peter for instance, Peter did exactly what he promised Jesus he would never do. He denied Jesus not once, not twice, but **three** times! Bible said Peter wept bitterly because the minute the roaster crowed, he remembered Jesus' words to him (Mark 14:66-72)
Apostle Paul can attest to this, he wrote in Romans 7:15-17;
"I don't really understand myself, for I want to do what is right, but I don't do it. Instead, I do what I hate. But if I know that what I am doing is wrong, this shows that I agree that the law is good. So I am not the one doing wrong; it is sin living in me that does it"

From having our faith tested, to sin controlling our actions; many of us suffer from constant trials and temptations, many of us gets our faith tested daily and that's why our daily prayer should be for God to strengthen our faith in Him.
We must live our God-given lives, knowing that our God is SOVEREIGN and His WORD is a powerful tool that can move mountains with faith even as small as a mustard seed.

It is my prayer that this book will make you stronger when you are weak, will strengthen your faith in God when your faith gets tested to the point of wanting to give up, will ultimately save your life when you don't see the point in living and will draw you to God if you don't know God or if you have been estranged from God.

This is your year of BLESSINGS, DIVINE BREAKTHROUGH AND AWESOME MIRACLES my friend! Don't let the blessings pass you by. There's NO room for failure and doubt.

God is behind the wheel. Enjoy the ride.

Trust God completely.

ABOUT THE AUTHOR

Evangelist Naomi Mensah Antwi is a humble servant of God, an entrepreneur, an author, a mother, a wife and a speaker with a heart for helping others and ministering the word of God. She is also the founder and CEO of Women for Christ International-WCI - a 501(c) 3 nonprofit Charity Ministry.

Learn more about Evangelist Naomi and her ministry on her website www.naomiantwi.com and check out her Ministry's website www.womenfci.org Evangelist Naomi and her husband Stephen have been married for over eleven years and God has blessed them with two beautiful children. Evangelist Naomi would love to hear from you.

Contact:
Evangelist Naomi Mensah Antwi
Founder & CEO
Women for Christ International—WCI
P O Box, 1294
Stafford, TX 77497
USA

Email evangelistnaomi@yahoo.com

Websites: www.naomiantwi.com
www.naomiantwi.net
www.womenfci.org

www.ingramcontent.com/pod-product-compliance
Lightning Source LLC
Chambersburg PA
CBHW071424090426
42737CB00011B/1556
* 9 7 8 0 6 9 2 7 5 3 0 5 7 *